A Drag Queen's Guide to Life

'MAGIC! A fun, fierce, honest origin story of how to drag yourself up out of trouble and become an icon' Katherine Ryan

'Eye-opening, intelligent and thoughtful as well as sassy and surprising – a must-read' Lorraine Kelly

'This book does many things: it educates, explains, describes and shares personal experiences, but all of that goodness is wrapped up in a beautiful layer of genuine kindness and care for the reader, who is possibly young, coming out and in some way or another exploring gender. Full of wit, wisdom and warmth' Juno Roche, author of *Trans Power* and *Queer Sex*

'Seeing Bimini take the world by storm with their authenticity, power and brilliance is truly a delight to see. *A Drag Queen's Guide to Life* is quintessential Bimini, hitting the nail on the head with their irreverent wit and infectious personality. Ms Boulash, you're definitely in the history books now!' Jamie Windust, author of *In Their Shoes*

'Bimini has written a book that mixes the personal, political, humour and glamour that surrounds them. A triumph for UK queer culture, this book welcomes their new audience into the queer present and past, with a clear argument for a gender-fluid future. It felt like it was part diary entry, part history lecture and part recording from a real good chat in a smoking area in east London – the best combination for a book!' Travis Alabanza, award-winning writer, performer and theatre-maker

'Bimini is absolutely brilliant in the way they are able to deliver such importantly crucial lessons about sexuality and gender in such a relatable and understanding way. *A Drag Queen's Guide to Life* is a very important read for so many of us out there who struggle with sexuality, gender and anything in between!' Gottmik

'A beautifully vulnerable and heartfelt journey from this down-to-earth high femme them. Bimini's radically real personal story reminds me to stay in my truth. This is a friendly reminder of self-love, and that your greatest gift to this world is to be yourself' Fox Fisher, artist, filmmaker, campaigner and author of *Trans Teen Survival Guide*

'The Queen has spoken and here are their Ten Queer Commandments. Radical, life-affirming and utterly important for this time. Bimini's wisdom and fresh outlook on gender identity and societal constraints are tackled with humanity and hilarity. A must-read for all Queers and those who care about them' Riyadh Khalaf

'With the generosity of spirit, wit and hilarity that we came to love from Bimini on *Drag Race*, their book is a triumphant celebration of living authentically – deftly combining the personal and the political, Bimini paints a picture of the world where we can all live freely. I enjoyed it immensely' Amrou Al-Kadhi, author of *Life as a Unicorn*

'It's easy to see why Bimini inspires so many people, injecting positivity where we need it. This book is Ru Paul's mantra "If you don't love yourself, how in the hell you gonna love somebody else?" updated and expanded upon for a new generation' Amelia Abraham, author of *Queer Intentions* and *We Can Do Better Than This*

'. . . and the next literary superstar is . . . Bimini Bon Boulash!!! Like the queen themselves – witty, hilarious, empowering – you will fall in love with *A Drag Queen's Guide to Life*!' Charlie Craggs, author of *To My Trans Sisters*

ABOUT THE AUTHOR

Bimini Bon Boulash is a drag performer from east London and finalist on *RuPaul's Drag Race UK*. As a model, Bimini has taken part in campaigns for Selfridges, Calvin Klein and Maison Margiela, alongside editorials for *British Vogue*, *Interview*, *Notion*, *Dazed*, *ES Magazine*, *W* and *Face*. Their debut single, 'God Save This Queen', was released in June 2021 and premiered on BBC Radio 1. They were born and raised in Great Yarmouth, Norfolk, and invented veganism about seven years ago.

BIMINI

BON BOULASH

A DRAG QUEEN'S GUIDE TO LIFE

PENGUIN BOOKS

PENGUIN BOOKS

UK | USA | Canada | Ireland | Australia
India | New Zealand | South Africa

Penguin Books is part of the Penguin Random House group of companies
whose addresses can be found at global.penguinrandomhouse.com.

Penguin
Random House
UK

First published as *Release the Beast* by Viking 2021
First published as *A Drag Queen's Guide to Life* in Penguin Books 2022

002

Text copyright © Bimini Bon Boulash, 2021
Illustrations copyright © Jules Scheele, 2021

The moral right of the copyright holders has been asserted

Typeset by Jouve (UK), Milton Keynes
Printed and bound in Great Britain by Clays Ltd, Elcograf S.p.A.

The authorized representative in the EEA is Penguin Random House Ireland,
Morrison Chambers, 32 Nassau Street, Dublin D02 YH68

A CIP catalogue record for this book is available from the British Library

ISBN: 978-0-241-54358-0

www.greenpenguin.co.uk

I'd like to dedicate this book to my mum. When I told you I was going to become a drag queen instead of using my degree in journalism you thought I was bonkers. Well, I've written a book with Penguin *and* I looked glamorous while I did it. I told you it was going to be worth it! I love you. Thank you for everything you've done, even when I was being a nightmare. X

Contents

Introduction:
Not a Joke, Just a Fact

Bimini Bon Book Author? You'd better bloody believe it, babes.

If you've picked this book up and started reading, you probably already know who I am (or maybe you're just a pervert with the hots for the bad bitch on the cover . . .).

You might have sat front row at one of my drag performances at The Glory in the early days, or watched me being crowned Miss Sink The Pink, or more likely you saw me strutting down the catwalk on *RuPaul's Drag Race* Season 2 dressed as a slutty Norwich City football player, in a suit covered in acne, or in the guise of an amoeba. Never say I don't have range.

This book is an absolute 'don't wake me if I'm dreaming' moment for me. I realised after being on a mainstream TV show that it was crucial for me to use my new

platform to speak up and shine a light on topics and political issues that were really important to me, both inside and outside of the LGBTQ+ community. Now here I am, a couple months later, with a book deal from Penguin Books (pinch me) and the incredible opportunity to write something that I wish I'd had in my hands growing up as a confused, gender nonconforming, queer kid in a small English seaside town.

Self-help books don't usually cater for people like me – they're usually written with a certain reader in mind, and that reader ain't queer, non-binary or working class. They're also very prescriptive – stick to this diet, order your pants drawer this way, fit into this box and people will love you. I've written this book as an antidote to all that. Think of it as an anti-self-help book – a radical and affirming self-love manifesto based on ten transformative life lessons that I have learned through the art of drag.

My aim with this book is to encourage the celebration of nonconformity in *all* of its senses, to give you the confidence to flip order and convention on their heads in your own life, and teach you how to live outside of society's definition of 'normal' (whatever the fuck that is!). Ultimately, if you feel like you don't fit in, this book has been written to empower you and encourage you to always be kind to yourself – no matter what.

So, that's why I'm writing – in the hope that this book opens up the minds of readers across the gender spectrum, inspires kindness and helps any queers out there – young and old – who are struggling with their identity. Drag gave me the confidence to get up on stage, perform and do the things I'd always dreamed of doing. It was an empowering gateway into the exploration of my own gender identity. Hopefully, the valuable lessons I have learned from drag over the years will help everyone reading this book to live the life they want to lead – no matter who they are. Nothing is out of reach!

After coming out as non-binary on TV in an open and light-hearted conversation with UK drag legend Ginny Lemon about gender and nonconformity, I was overwhelmed and inspired by the support and kindness in the responses online and in the media. Topics like this very rarely receive any kind of thoughtful coverage in the mainstream media. We had managed to break through the cis-tem just a little bit and shatter some of the misconceptions about being non-binary and gender nonconforming (and even inspired some people to come out to their friends and family – incredible!). *A Drag Queen's Guide to Life* is my way of sharing the joy, power and strength that is to be found in not conforming – in the broadest sense possible. The life-changing magic of dragging up is very real and it's for *everyone*.

In the following pages I share stories from my own life and personal struggles with gender and identity, as well as the stories of many of the wonderful nonconformist, convention-breaking icons that have inspired and helped to create the Bimini Bon Boulash that you see on the cover – from fellow drag queens and kings, to musicians, gender theorists, fashion designers and more.

These ten lessons will guide you through everything

I've learned from my experience of drag and applied to my own life, from how to embrace the femme, dismantle the patriarchy and be a cis-tem offender, to the importance of knowing your her-story; how to navigate the worlds of fashion and fitness as an outsider; how to develop a positive mental attitude and, most importantly, how to love yourself – he, she or them. Class is in session!

When you put this book down, I hope you come away with the confidence to be your authentic self, to challenge nonsensical norms and binaries, to not conform, to celebrate difference, and to live outside of society's bizarre boxes. It's okay to mess up, we're all human and we're definitely not all perfect. Take it from me, the best art comes from fucking up, learning to laugh at yourself and going against the grain. We'll all get there, eventually!

So to all of the nonconformists, gender benders and cis-tem offenders out there, to anyone reading this book who feels like they don't fit in – this is for you.

It's time to release the beast.

Death drop

The life-changing *MAGIC* of DRAGGING UP is very REAL ~ and it's for EVERYONE!!

Life Lesson 1:
Don't Be Scared to Embrace the Femme

The idea of drag fascinated me the moment I first saw it. I viewed it as an expression and celebration of femininity (or masculinity for drag kings, although the two aren't mutually exclusive – I'll be explaining more about all this later on), which wasn't something I had been able to celebrate in my previous life without feeling shame or guilt. There was an intrinsic confidence that I longed for.

Perhaps naively, I saw all the good in drag immediately and ignored the issues with some parts of the drag world that shouldn't be ignored: like the fact that some forms of drag can be misogynistic – something I hope to tackle head-on in this book. But back then the 18-year-old queer kid who knew deep down that a strict gender binary didn't resonate with my own experience saw drag as a gateway to the exploration of my own gender identity.

Despite being labelled a boy when I was born, I was always drawn to femininity. My earliest memories all have women playing the starring roles. If my early life were a movie, men were mere extras while women took the lead, the supporting roles, and were directing and producing too. Women ran shit in the world I grew up in. My babysitter and her daughter, my mum's best friends' children, my

7

friends at playgroup, my mother, my grandmother, my auntie – the list could go on. I was always around female energy.

I was also what you might call an attention seeker. I remember getting Remi, my mum's friend's daughter, to cover me head-to-toe in gloss paint while I paraded around completely nude, like I was an art installation at the V&A. Our mums found it hilarious, although they did tell us both off so that we wouldn't do it again. We wasted an entire pot making my skin glow like I'd just been on a photoshoot in *Hunger* magazine. I think people warmed to the idea that I was an attention seeker very early on. It was cute because I was young, but as I got older, I became more socially aware, knowing that expressing femininity as a boy would earn me ridicule.

One of the things I would do was create a rota at playgroup so that I could get my way of being in charge of who wore the pearl necklace and the dress that day. I was not only an attention seeker, but a boss bitch from a young age. Nobody could tell me what I was doing was wrong, although my mum tells me the playgroup staff found themselves immersed in controversy when parents would come to pick up their children and be outraged at Tommy, aged three, looking drop-dead gorgeous in a purple velvet dress. My mum always supported the idea, thankfully, because it obviously made me happy. That's what parents ultimately want, right? A smile on their child's face. When you're young and you're developing, your environment is a key factor but I think it's important to not look for reasons why a child is gender nonconforming – looking for a reason suggests there's something wrong. Some kids just are, and that's fine.

My mum has also had a huge influence on my understanding of femininity, as well as strength and resilience. When I was very young she was a single mother, working her arse off to provide a better life for me. I grew up with a mum who was an incredibly independent woman. She didn't want to ever have to rely on a man because she knew she could rely on herself. Her work ethic is unparalleled and, as I grew up, I understood this. I'm eternally thankful for what she sacrificed to provide for me and, even better, she'd be doing it all in a heel. I always viewed my mum as glam, gorgeous and a go-getter. She's the strongest person I know, male, female, or somewhere in between.

Femininity can be powerful. I walked into Season 2 of *RuPaul's Drag Race UK* wearing a hot pink, faux leather dominatrix-inspired outfit with 'vegan bitch' studded on the front panels, paired with pink diamante nipples.

I wore it with big, voluminous blonde hair and knee-high marble pink stripper boots (by an iconic East London designer called Natasha Marrow) and I had one goal in mind – for people to write me off as a serious competitor because of how I looked. I played up to stereotypical views of femininity and manufactured the idea that I would just be a bimbo for the viewers watching and for my fellow competitors. This was all part of a cunning plan to make people underestimate me – just as femininity is hugely underestimated. *Drag Race* was the city of Troy and my bimbo persona was a Trojan Horse; once I infiltrated the city borders (the workroom), I wanted to destroy all the preconceived ideas people had about me and my talents. Turns out I was capable of more than looking a little bit blonde and a whole lot of sexy.

Let's just consider the bimbo stereotype for a moment, shall we? A bimbo traditionally means a woman that has nothing much else of value beyond her sexy looks. Depending on who you ask, 'bimbo' can be seen as a neutral description or a nasty insult. But who gets to define who or what a bimbo is?

In fact, the word bimbo actually comes from the Italian word 'bambino' which means male baby. The feminine version would be 'bimba'. Originally a bimbo referred to a foolish or insignificant man, but rapidly changed to mean a woman in the latter half of the twentieth century. That shift says a lot, right? How come a term with a negative connotation about masculinity got passed on and instead became associated with femininity? Misogyny, probably.

Hollywood movies in the 1950s and 1960s developed the bimbo stereotype into the form we know today. You can trace the evolution of the bimbo in Julie Holliday's performance in *Born Yesterday* and, famously, in the work of Marilyn Monroe. Bimbo film characters were often referred to as simple or treated like babies with their high-pitched, breathy voices. In these movies quite often the bimbo's high standards of sexuality were unobtainable, or difficult for other women to live up to. The bimbo would be above other women in her sex appeal but the pay-off was that she was beneath other women in her intellect.

In the 1980s and 1990s, the term bimbo was commonly used in descriptions of scandals involving politicians or public figures. The *Baltimore Sun* published an article titled 'Lewinsky being branded a Bimbo' in reference to the political scandal of her affair with Bill Clinton. Naturally, in these headlines it was always the women that were assigned the term bimbo over the men, although they were most likely victims of powerful men (the patriarchy, duh).

I've grown up socially conscious but with a finger on the pulse of pop culture and have been intrigued by how men and the media (which is mostly run by men) treat famous women, and how even different language is used to describe men and women. It's always interested me how some women in the public eye will play up to the male gaze by using the persona of a bimbo even when it is plain to see that they are both intelligent and self-aware.

Is it cold in here or is it just my nipples? Even the queen of the tabloids, the Pricey, started her career by feeding into the male gaze, all while going on to become a hugely successful businesswoman with ventures in almost every avenue possible. Katie spoke to BBC2 for its 2020 documentary *Celebrity: A 21st-Century Story* and on camera she explained this has always been intentional: 'What I am is shrewd. I act stupid, but I know what's going on.'

This was what I wanted to do. I wanted to be underestimated so that I could prove people wrong. I knew what was going on; nobody else did.

On the show my bimbo persona almost didn't work because I nearly went home (imagine!) in episode one, but in the long run it bagged me a book deal with Penguin Books. Now I'm lying here on a writer's retreat in Margate,

eating vegan croissants and drinking freshly squeezed orange juice, looking out at the sun glinting on the sea. I won.

I've always admired women who were both their own version of feminine and strong-minded, and bosses in a male-dominated world (my mother being a great example of a working-class woman who went on to own two businesses). A lot of celebrities have played into this idea of femininity over the years. Dolly Parton, who has a song titled 'Dumb Blonde' where she pokes fun at the bimbo persona, famously spoke on the subject in a 1977 interview with Barbara Walters. When asked about her outlandish outfits she said, 'I just decided that I would do something that would at least get the attention . . . once they got past the shock of the ridiculous way I looked they would see there were parts of me to be appreciated . . . I know they make fun of me. All these years people have thought the joke was on me but actually the joke was on the public. Because I know exactly what I'm doing and I can change it at any time'. For me this is nothing short of iconic. Queen Dolly has been manipulating the public since the 1970s and she's still popping today. All hail Dolly Parton. She basically funded one of the COVID-19 vaccines as well. Love that for her.

Thanks to the young kids making waves on TikTok, a lot of videos have been pushing a similar agenda to my own idea, which is about reclaiming femininity outside of the male gaze. If you haven't heard of it before, the 'male gaze' is a concept first suggested by the English art critic John Berger in 1972 in his landmark BBC film series *Ways of Seeing* and then popularised by the feminist film critic Laura Mulvey. Basically, the idea is that for centuries women have only ever been depicted in art, literature and film as objects for the pleasure of a heterosexual male viewer. TikTok content creators like Chrissy Chlapecka are part of a new wave of women subverting that male gaze by playing up to the bimbo stereotype on camera while asserting their own feminist politics. Chlapecka has said 'the bimbo is pro-choice, pro-sex work, pro-BLM and she, he, or they likes to look pretty. We like to look pretty while we're doing it.' Too bloody right! GOD SAVE THE BIMBO!

Growing up in a small seaside town as male presenting, expectations for how I wanted to live didn't always meet reality. Much to the dismay of the other children, I knew I had the ability to fulfil all five roles of the Spice Girls without the need for extras. Unfortunately I did have to allow extras into the scenario, which meant I would often end up starring in the role of Ginger. My fiery red hair being the perfect colour co-ord to play the

character. As the only boy in the lineup, I took it upon myself to show everyone else up. This was often met with snide remarks from teachers but I didn't care, I believed I was destined to be in a girl group but I was unaware of the restraints I would face by what was between my legs. In the fantasy of my blossoming pop career, I was never Ed Sheeran. The world pictured me in a different way than I viewed myself. The comments about my hair colour were irrelevant when parents would refer to me as the gay one *does camp hand gesture* way before I even knew what that meant. It's tricky understanding adults when you're finding it difficult to know where you're going wrong. I realise now I wasn't going wrong, everyone else was playing the role that had been assigned to them. Society tried to repress this innate femininity but it didn't work. I think this forced me to become aware early on that I was different. I thought maybe I was gonna be a witch.

Throughout history, children tagged as male who identified with femininity were thought to be delusional or disturbed. Obviously, we are hopefully moving into a time where most people realise that mental illness has absolutely nothing to do with it. Reading fashion magazines and being infatuated with feminine silhouettes didn't mean I was mentally ill or disturbed. If we lived in a society where gender constraints on children didn't exist, we would push further as a society towards true equality. Femininity is widely criticised as a weakness; to be feminine as a boy you're subject to ridicule, which only proves that femininity is seen as weaker than masculinity.

In my first look on *Drag Race*, I embraced the view of femininity that is widely recognised to be attractive to the straight man, so that I could then go on to subvert gender stereotypes by showing the fluidity of gender and expression of sexual identity. In my second look in that premiere episode, I stepped out on to the runway wearing a high-rise Norwich City Football Club leotard with 10-inch thigh-highs and a rugged blonde mullet, looking not unlike the club's former star striker Darren Huckerby.

I was playing into both masculinity and femininity here, inspired by the football hooliganism that is typically asso-ciated with macho, violent, working-class culture but adding hyper-feminine elements to it, completely flipping the script. Wearing an outfit that shouldn't be worn on the main stage of *Drag Race* was an attempt to subvert gender ideals. I would go to football matches as a teenager during a time when I was trying to fit in with the masculine stand-ards of those around me. I was trying to fit in, okay! I was ginger with acne and braces; I couldn't be a rampantly gender nonconforming 14-year-old as well! Jokes aside,

that Norwich City outfit was slept on at the time and I still stand by it. If you don't want to take my word for it, they're only putting it on exhibition in an actual museum in Norwich. It was ahead of its time, I promise!

Earlier on I spoke about drag queens creating looks using femininity and drag kings doing the same using masculinity, although neither are exclusive to one another. As that Norwich City look showed, you can still be a drag queen and play with the aesthetics of masculinity. However, I am sure that there will be plenty of people reading – of all gender identities – who just don't feel femininity resonates with them at all, or even makes them personally feel uncomfortable – and that's totally valid too! Processing our own relationship to gender isn't always easy and all our experiences can be different. This is where the idea of gender being a spectrum comes in. Someone who is crushing the cis-tem on mainstream television is *RuPaul's Drag Race* Season 13 contestant Gottmik. What Mik is doing for gender nonconformity is incredible. He's a trans man who is also playing around with the full spectrum of gender by showcasing femininity and androgyny as a drag queen. It's pretty incredible and I'm sure it'd be mind-blowing for some gammon-faced types who don't really understand transness or queerness. Mik is completely flipping the script on gender nonconformity in the most punk rock way, and it's inspiring.

As someone who has watched the queer scene in East London change pretty rapidly, I am thankful that I've always been part of a world where gender was never

questioned; where what's between your legs was no one else's business. The Glory in East London is where my drag was birthed, as well as an array of alternative queer talent. There no one bats a cheap, clumpy fake eyelash. I'm lucky enough to have found my home in a community where gender binaries are challenged, not reinforced.

When I ask my family members what their idea of drag is, they automatically picture a drag queen, and that drag queen is always viewed as a man in a wig. It's often seen as comedic and a stereotype when, in fact, the drag I've been surrounded by in East London is all about pushing boundaries and fighting those stereotypes. Drag kings and other gender nonconforming artists within the East London circuit that I've had the pleasure of working with such as Chiyo, Adam All, Prinx Silver and Beau Jangles all use their performance style to push a message of their own struggles, pain, identity and sexuality. There is no box that drag can be fit into anymore. We're ever evolving!

The point is that gender IS a spectrum. I'm going to try and break down what I mean by that in as simple a way as I can. I believe masculinity and femininity are fluid. I believe there are levels and varying degrees of both. What are the key stereotypes of masculinity and femininity? On a basic level, masculinity is strength, leadership, assertiveness. Femininity is nurturing, emotional, sensitive. When associated with their assigned gender roles, society thinks it's fine, but when you flip them there becomes an issue. A woman that is seen as strong threatens a man. A man that is seen as sensitive is viewed as weak. After unleashing a ferocious verse on Kanye's 'Monster' where, and god

forbid, three men were out-rapped by a FEMALE, Nicki Minaj, wearing a Marge Simpson-esque pink wig said: 'When a man is assertive, he's called a boss; when I'm assertive I'm called a bitch!' These double standards leak out into the rest of society.

I'm gonna dive in even deeper. Get ready . . .

Let's think about sex assignment at birth. When you're born, a box is ticked for you saying whether you are going to grow up to be male or female. You're then dressed in a pink or blue towel and your family pretends you're the cutest thing that's ever blessed this planet when in fact we all look like shrivelled grapes. You are expected to keep on living your life from this point on under the pretence that you are a number and not an individual. People often don't quite grasp the difference between sex and gender. It's tricky, I get it. It doesn't help that they're often used interchangeably, despite having different meanings. So let's give it a go.

'Sex' refers to a cluster of biological attributes in humans. Things like our reproductive/sexual anatomy, chromosomes and hormones. This is where we're categorised as 'female' or 'male'. But there can be a difference in attributes that determine sex and how they are expressed. Typically a foetus during a pre-natal scan or a newborn baby (depending on how impatient the parents are to know) are attributed a sex based only on one characteristic: genitalia (because it can be seen). From that point we are given a birth certificate with male or female on it and sent off to live our lives.

'Gender' refers to the socially constructed roles created by society that determine the behaviours, expressions and identities of boys, men, girls, women and gender nonconforming people. It varies from culture to culture and can change over time. It has a strong influence over how we perceive ourselves and each other and also how we act, interact and the power we are given in society. My view is that gender identity is not fixed nor is it confined to a binary; it flows between the two and exists in a sequence that can change over time. There is so much interpretation in the understanding of gender identity and how we as humans understand, experience and play into gender through the roles we take on.

When I was in high school I didn't have much going for me in terms of physical attractiveness. I was short, had braces, acne and glasses and I was also blessed with being a carrot top. It's true: I'm a natural ginger. My sexuality developed quite early considering I looked like a knee and I experimented with it before realising that my sexuality was fluid as well. It seemed easier to fall into attraction to men, or at least the idea of a man. I think sexuality and gender are tricky conversations to have with wider audiences because we've all thought about poking a variety of people, and fantasies, desires and attractions can change over time. We've all got an understanding of what it is to be lesbian, gay or bisexual when it comes to sexuality, but as human beings and language are forever evolving, new words, terms and reclaimed insults are being added, just to confuse those that are content to be normies and stay thinking in binaries (sorry, huns).

An example of a recent evolution in language about sexuality is 'pansexual', a term used to describe someone who is not limited in their sexual attractions in regard to biological gender, sex or gender identity. Queer has become an umbrella term for anyone that fits in the 'other' category of the LGBTQ+ acronym. It shouldn't be forgotten that a lot of older LGBTQ+ activists have a problem with the word queer because they experienced it in its original meaning – as a slur – while the generation I've grown up in have sought to proudly reclaim it. I can view it as a form of empowerment but I understand that isn't for everyone.

Much like how the term bimbo evolved (or devolved?) from an insult aimed at men to one aimed at women, the way in which we express gender to the world is always changing and has done throughout history. All the way back in the tenth century high-heeled shoes were first worn by men to help keep their shoes in stirrups – '6 Inch' [Heels] was actually written first for the Persian cavalry but it was too emotional so they passed it on to Beyoncé – and actually over the centuries a lot of clothes were gender-neutral. Jo Paoletti, author of *Pink and Blue: Telling the Girls from the Boys in America* says that for centuries, children wore dainty white dresses up to the age of six: 'What was once a matter of practicality – you dress your baby in white dresses and diapers; white cotton can be bleached – became a matter of "Oh my God, if I dress my baby in the wrong thing, they'll grow up perverted".'

So what the hell has changed? It ain't that bloody long ago! Why was I shunned at nursery because even though I looked drop-dead gorgeous in my purple velour dress, the other fathers and mothers alike found it terrible? Was it a threat that I was being free? Was me prancing around thinking I was Dorothy from *The Wizard of Oz* going to do *so* much harm?

Again, thank the heavens for the youth. Whitney was right: the kids really are the future. The youngest generation is proving to be the most tolerant and fluid, and this is being documented all over social media and TikTok. Same-sex couples and numerous sexual identities have been given more of a platform throughout the media (*Drag Race* being one!), but there is still a long way to go to reach full diversity. A study by Ipsos Mori stated that only 66 per cent of young people identity as exclusively heterosexual. Now if that ain't some satanic statistic, I don't know what is . . . and you know what? I LOVE IT!

Things are becoming more fluid. After all, the generation that birthed me (and gave rise to the rapid destruction of the planet), AKA the baby boomers, make up the highest percentage of those identifying as heterosexual at 88 per cent. This change can be linked to a more tolerant society when it comes to sexuality and to gender. Basically, the future is genderless, and I'm so ready for it.

Debate, like lettuce, is healthy. Discussions are important. But I'd say we're still in a time where these topics are discussed in a climate of intimidation and humiliation, rather than in environments which are honest and fair. So much conflict could be avoided if we were open to perspectives radically different from our own.

THE FUTURE IS GENDERLESS ...AND I'M SO READY FOR IT !

We're not all fighting the same fight but we're fighting a common enemy – the patriarchy. Unless you're a straight, cis, white wealthy male you've likely had experiences that demonstrate the control and power the patriarchy has over you. Whether it's an older family member at a Christmas dinner being biphobic, or a boss at work that might make an inappropriate sexual remark that we know is unacceptable now (it never wasn't, but some of us have shifted our consciousness to know that slapping a colleague's arse without consent is NOT acceptable), we've all witnessed toxic masculinity, whether consciously or subconsciously. The patriarchy is responsible for unrealistic beauty standards and the oppression of women, children and LGBTQ+ members, not to mention greed and the abuse of money and power. In short, the patriarchy is responsible for all the evil we're trying to combat in the world. I am a firm believer that women and gender nonconforming individuals should run the world. Beyoncé manifested it; now it's time to put it into action.

I'd even extend this by saying that although they hugely benefit from being white men, working-class men are used for labour for the patriarchy, usually working month by month to fill the pockets of the wealthy and made examples of when it comes to crime statistics, when actually there is a whole lot of crime happening at an elite level that gets brushed to the side. I don't have to make any royal examples because I'm sure you could guess who I might be talking about.

Privilege is like a multitiered (non-vegan) cake, as there are layers to privilege and people may not realise theirs because it's never been discussed or questioned. I might be a gender nonconforming individual but I was also born white and British and I have, at times, done things in my life to try and pass as a straight, white man (although I was hugely uncomfortable and, on reflection, there ain't nobody I was fooling). Still, when I did it made things a whole lot bloody easier. Fundamentally, it's about understanding and empathising with the experiences of others and how that may go against your own individual experience and that's okay. Be open to listening to other people's feelings rather than shutting them down because they're different to your own.

Every single time we come together in this fight, we're chipping away at a cis-tem created to benefit no one other than the patriarchy. This links to all forms of oppression, including homophobia, transphobia, sexism and racism, as well as the environmental destruction and exploitation of our planet.

I believe our generation can crush this patriarchal

cis-tem. If we fight to reclaim our own bodies, we will regain our humanity and we'll look back in history and be outraged at how long we accepted the Western idea of the gender binary being so strict. The patriarchy exists because an elite group has engineered the idea of a gender binary without resistance. First religion and now the media are using manipulative tools to keep gender binary alive so that it can benefit the patriarchy. So let's talk about fighting it!

Life Lesson 2:
Be a Cis-Tem Offender

Picture this. You're sitting in your Sociology A-Level lesson. Your tutor is discussing the importance of social sciences and how understanding how the world works is important for our progression. They discuss great books such as *The Art of War* by Sun Tzu, *A Vindication of the Rights of Woman* by Mary Wollstonecraft, *The Communist Manifesto* by Marx and Engels, and the hottest manifesto, *A Drag Queen's Guide to Life* by Bimini Bon Boulash. A masterpiece in the discussion of gender politics. Every age in history has had its defining political text arguing for how best to change society for the better. Basically, Karl Marx walked so I could strut. I wonder if Karl wore heels?

In the last chapter, I shared a couple of anecdotes about my life and introduced some very basic concepts about gender being constructed and how it can be fluid. Identity can constantly change and there is no one rule when it comes to gender, but alas, my idea of a world where we dance around drinking the tears of a crushed patriarchy seems far removed from where we actually are in society. I want to talk about the systems that harm all of us, particularly toxic media, and the importance of resisting these by having discussions and challenging inequality in all areas of our lives.

Before all that though, I think now's the time to get

further into the grit of core terms and identities that are central to the drag world Bimini comes from, but are still confusing to people new to it. Because a lack of education can lead to prejudice (without pride).

I've briefly mentioned sex and gender. One is assigned to you when you're born based on physical characteristics, and the other is a set of socially constructed ideas or norms which shape how we understand ourselves. This is important because it relates to the definitions of words like 'trans', 'non-binary' and 'gender nonconforming' and it's also central to understanding what 'drag' as an art form is about. All these concepts are very different but do have some overlap (and some tensions) which I'm keen to unpack – so let's get into it!

First of all, the term 'trans' is an umbrella term (you can stand under my umbrella ella ella etc.) used to describe anyone who feels that their own gender identity (how they see and experience their gender) is different to or doesn't sit comfortably with the sex they were assigned at birth. You've probably heard of trans people who transition from male to female (trans women – think of someone like Peppermint from *Drag Race* in the US or Hunter Schafer in HBO teen series *Euphoria*), or vice versa, using hormones and surgery; stories about these kinds of people have been in the media for years. While this is the most visible kind of trans person, not every trans person will want surgery or even hormones. If you were assigned female at birth but identify as male you are a trans man (like Gottmik who we met in the last chapter) and that's that, whether you take testosterone or not. Your medical history doesn't determine your gender: you do.

However, also under the larger trans umbrella we have people who don't want to cross the binary from male to female or female to male, or who feel they sit between the two or shift between them. This group encompasses a massive spectrum of identities and experiences so we use a catch-all term for them called 'non-binary' (hi!). Non-binary people can look and present in all sorts of different ways but if they like to play with their gender expression in a way that society tends to view as unusual for how 'men' or 'women' should look, they may also identify as 'gender nonconforming' (hi again). So I'm Tommy and I was assigned male at birth but I sit under the trans umbrella because I am non-binary and gender nonconforming. Keeping up?

So if we have trans people (everyone under the full trans umbrella still adds up to less than 1 per cent of the population) we need a word for everyone who doesn't identify as trans, right? A word that isn't bloody 'normal'. That's why, since the 1990s, the term 'cisgender' has grown in popularity, now often shortened to 'cis'. 'Transgender' basically means 'across, on the other side of gender' in Latin, while 'cisgender' means 'on this side of gender'. Basically, for those of us who aren't Classics professors sat in tweed jackets, cis means the opposite to trans. If your gender feels the same as the one listed as your sex on your birth certificate, you're cis. That's why I call it the 'cis-tem', because we still live in a world where many people wrongly assume everyone is cis. Another word that you might not have heard before if you don't know any trans people is 'dysphoria'. It comes from the Greek for 'sad' but in a gender context refers to the profound feelings of unhappiness many trans people might feel with aspects of their bodies and how this causes society to perceive them. It's also a clinical term for when people medically transition: they may use hormones or surgery to alleviate their gender dysphoria. So here are the terms we've covered so far: assigned male at birth, assigned female at birth, cis, trans, non-binary, gender nonconforming, trans man, trans woman and dysphoria.

If that isn't spicy enough for you let's throw in another way to look at gender – drag. Spoiler alert: I'm a drag

queen while also being non-binary. Drag queens and trans people have a long and complicated history – existing often side by side or even overlapping, but sometimes with mutual suspicion and hostility. This suspicion often came from the fact that until the explosion of drag into the mainstream (thank you, *Drag Race*), Joe Public used to confuse drag queens with trans women. This was because of some pretty problematic stereotypes about both what trans women are and what drag queens are. To be crass: a lot of people just used to think 'same thing: man in a wig'. Hopefully – in case any of you are still hearing stuff like that around the family table – I can clear this up for you.

Drag is an art form and a performance. One that literally anyone can do – man, woman, non-binary. Trans person or cis person. I'm going to repeat that: EVERYONE can do drag. From my experience of coming up on the drag scene as an artist, I learned early on that drag went against the norms of how people are supposed to look, sound and be in their gender; it parodied, mocked and mirrored what was going on socially and politically. I understand this might not be the case for all types of drag, but even the idea that a woman doing drag pisses some people off – which it does – is, to me, punk as hell. A woman doing drag is a political statement . . . full stop. I've never understood why some people think that only a male body can become a drag queen and that if a woman or a non-binary person who was originally assigned female decides to call themselves a drag queen, it isn't drag.

Most men and people like me who get read as men by society claim to be doing drag because we are inspired by women. So how then can some in the community try to turn around and tell those same women they're not welcome in drag? It's pretty fucked up and totally misogynistic. Equally, sometimes drag scenes have been disrespectful to the struggles of trans people by refusing to be welcoming, even using slurs like the word 'tranny' – a hurtful insult – in the names of their events and nights.

For everyone to be able to enjoy the same opportunities, everybody should be invited into these discussions. We have to stand up against the cis-tem together. Drag artists and trans women and men have been at the forefront of demonstrations, protests and riots for gay rights and equality across the world (which we will talk about soon). Challenging the cis-tem of gender opens up a dialogue to question other things, like whether my arse looks great in this pair of second-hand Levis or whether the gender pay gap will ever be equal. It pushes us forward.

I also want us to start thinking about politics beyond gender and the LGBTQ+ scene, too. Now remember my mini-challenge quote about 52 per cent deceit and 48 per cent despair? The Brexit buns? Me making a Brexit-related joke on a *Drag Race* show? (Iconic.) Well scrap that because it was 100 per cent deceit and 100 per cent despair for all of us that voted to remain. Watching this steady rise of the right wing is terrifying, particularly in a country that is viewed worldwide as being pretty liberal. Maybe it isn't the country I once thought it was.

When I moved to London I guess I fell into part of the metropolitan elite, naive to the fearmongering that was going on and how isolated the rest of the United Kingdom felt, brought on by divisive tactics in the media. I made the move to London as it felt important for me to get a sense of freedom. But we can become so wrapped up in the community we build here that we forget that not everyone experiences the same things as us. I've never experienced wealth but now, since *Drag Race*, I've been catapulted into a world that wasn't necessarily designed for me. I'm being told I have to have a business advisor and start investing . . . but investing in what? If I ever make money, I want to be investing it into a better country that all of us can benefit from. I want to know that the taxes I pay are going into social and public services, and not nuclear weapons and warfare. I want the NHS, one of the greatest socialist inventions to grace this planet, to be fairly funded and not to be on its knees begging for more money and pandering to the Tories to sustain it.

Many of the queer kids who are reading this book right now may be stuck at home, living in a community (often regional) that doesn't allow them the freedom to be who they want to be. We're in a political mess due to divisive tactics, but throw in the consequences of a global pandemic and rising student debt, and you see that this is not fair for everyone and no one will be able to truly thrive or flourish unless they come from a place of financial privilege. When I moved to London in 2012, I noticed a drastic shift in inequality. Higher rent has moved me out of the inner parts of London and the cost of living in the capital is just ridiculous. We're a lot more unequal now than we've been in a long time and it shouldn't be underestimated how much harder that makes it to find your community. The past two years have been terrifying socially; the past six years have been terrifying politically.

What I want to try and tackle in this chapter is how we can all come together to challenge this inequality, and no, we don't have to wear daisy chains and dance around to Jefferson Airplane (no slight on Jefferson Airplane – Grace Slick is a psychedelic queen!).

I was a lucky little bugger as a child. I had flaming red hair, although my mum would call it golden to appease the ridicule and torment I was bound to endure. Let's not call it a royal colour, let's go with Celtic. I'd much rather be part of a Celtic bloodline with Boudicca, the queen of Iceni, than the current unelected elite.

Other than celebrating my golden locks, my mum gave me freedom when it came to being a bit of a gender nonconformist, despite cries from family members telling her I would grow up gay. (Sorry to disappoint you all but I've grown up to be a lot more than just that!)

It was so natural to me. I immediately gravitated to the ruby slippers Dorothy wore on *The Wizard of Oz*. Maybe I wanted to return to whatever galaxy had overcome the need for gender binaries. There was an innocence in me, like a young Britney Spears trying to navigate a world too corrupt for our purity. I wasn't delusional, nor was I naive. I've always been self-aware and from memory it was at around the age of seven or eight that I started

realising that my interests and actions weren't what was expected.

Much like many queer/gay children, I was a 'joy to have in class'. Is it me or is that always a euphemism for a raging homosexual? Whatever it was, my flamboyant nature did start to be chipped away. Slowly, with every dig or insult, that sparkle started to vanish.

I stopped creating pop groups with the girls and tried my hand at a popular sport, the one where men wearing tiny shorts are split into teams and they run around a field for 90 minutes kicking a ball into a net. Once the ball hits said net they scream GOAL! That means one point. This is a sport where men are encouraged to feel emotion. This is a sport where men are encouraged to FIGHT for their team. It brings them glory. They can cry if they want because it isn't being sensitive, it's because they feel so much passion for these men in shorts kicking a football into a net. It isn't seen as weakness, it's seen as strength.

My question is . . . why is it acceptable for men to feel so much emotion on the pitch but not in everyday life?

Ahh . . . Another example of social conditioning. If a bloke's football team loses and he's crying into his beer is he ever told to man up? Is he told to get on with it?

Social conditioning comes in all sorts of forms. It comes from other kids in schools, from our parents, grandparents, the media, advertising. It's unstoppable and subconsciously we take on what we see in the world around us. That's how the human psyche works. We adapt to what we're supposed to do in order to survive.

I'm not tooting my own horn, but for a white boy I could bust a move or two. I used to enter competitions, perform in big dance shows and quite often take home the golden trophy. But during my teenage years I remember hiding this from my peers until it reached a point where I told my mum I no longer wanted to dance, even though I loved to dance; it was where I truly felt free and creative. This pressure to conform did take a toll on me and I feel embarrassed to admit it.

Sadly, it doesn't stop with me. Stonewall did some studies and found out that:

- Nearly half of LGBT pupils (45 per cent) – including 64 per cent of trans pupils – are bullied for being LGBT in Britain's schools.
- Half of LGBT pupils hear homophobic slurs 'frequently' or 'often' at school, down from seven in ten in 2012.

These statistics are quite harrowing, but unsurprising. My mission is to keep fighting until it doesn't matter how or what you identify as. I want people to see us for the souls we have and the body as just a vessel which carries it.

To make these changes happen we have to challenge the cis-tem. There are various ways to do this. Firstly, we have to tackle education.

When I turned sixteen in high school I was made a prefect. I'm not quite sure if I deserved that title (the transition from me being a gifted pre-teen to a horrific, hormonal, weed-smoking teenager was drastic) but alas,

I was given authority. With great power came my decision to ignore the school jumper policy for boys and start wearing a navy cardigan like the girls. It was cuter. I wanted to wear a cardigan. I felt more femme.

Can you imagine the outrage? Isolation. Eye rolls and tuts from the teachers. How dare I break the rules and wear a CARDIGAN as a BOY?

It wasn't until the school rules were looked into and there was nothing in them that stated that boys couldn't opt for a soft navy cardigan if they should want to. Through gritted teeth I was allowed to continue trailblazing in my George cardigan and slowly but surely I saw the younger boys in school start wearing cardigans too. I'm pretty sure they all turned out to be on the LGBTQ+ spectrum, but then again, who isn't? Regardless, I won a small battle for femmekind and now I'm fighting in a worldwide battle for us ALL to be accepted.

Before going on to television stardom as a drag artist, I studied for a BA degree in journalism. I started on fashion journalism because I thought I wanted to write about fancy clothes and my favourite designers, but then I went on to do a degree in broad journalism, with the option of choosing the route I wanted to go down.

This was when I started to learn the history of the printing press, the media and how manipulative and brainwashing it can be. The media is usually run by an elite group of powerful men that control the narrative of society politics by inducing moral panics. We've seen how the media is often incredibly sexist and outrageously homophobic and has a huge role in sustaining patriarchal control over us. The British tabloids enforce pretty much every single form of prejudice possible, whether it's mocking the poor, or continually using racist rhetoric and shaming working-class people.

We should look to the mainstream media as a way to start fighting against the cis-tem and its agenda.

I'm obviously a big old vegan leftie but witnessing the harassment and propaganda against Jeremy Corbyn was the first time I felt emotionally and politically intelligent enough to really see the agenda that was being pushed. A man like Corbyn was never going to get into power because he threatened the elitist status quo that had been built upon for hundreds of years. A socialist through and through, he would have put his heart and soul into doing what he thought was right. He had integrity – so he had to go.

It's not just politics; it's celebrity culture too. I was a teenager at a time when pop culture was popping. We had flip phones, social media was starting, celebrities were playing with the media and giving us everything we wanted and more. I know a lot of young queer kids who were teens in the early 2000s who felt the same way – we glorified the idea of a tragic woman because that was the narrative that was being pushed at the time. The iconic image of Britney, Lindsay and Paris in the car 'broke the internet' before that was a thing. Lindsay Lohan going off the rails was an obsession for me and, perhaps, I felt a sense of identification with that.

If you look at how vilification by the media happens, it's usually women and people who identify as LGBTQ+

that get the harshest edits: Cishet men walk away scar free. Think about how it's often easier for men to make a comeback after experiencing distress or breakdowns in public. In recent years we saw Ant (of Ant and Dec) being welcomed back into the mainstream with open arms because he'd been through a lot of personal problems and trauma, but famous women with similar issues don't get the same opportunity for redemption. Lindsay Lohan was shunned and her entire career ruined because she sought rehabilitation and wasn't lucky enough to get it when she needed it.

Gossip magazines create propaganda and smear people every day. Tabloid queen Katie Price has lies about her spread across the front covers weekly. If a man is ever on the cover of one of these magazines, he's usually topless and it's a positive story about how he's saved a kitten from a tree or something. But god forbid the papers ever celebrate Katie Price getting married again.

I hate to admit it but I became addicted to Britney's meltdown. Watching Amy Winehouse self-destruct was brought to us as a form of entertainment. On reflection how awful do I feel that I ate up what the media was

45

feeding? At the time it was so normalised and ingrained in our culture that we were conditioned into thinking it was acceptable. Power to those that stood up against the media then because I know I didn't. In fact, it possibly inspired me to start taking drugs because I thought it was glamorous. Go figure.

The media coaches us to laugh at young women in distress and this creates a toxic culture of misogyny and femmephobia; it's no surprise that they haven't welcomed transgender and gender nonconforming people with open arms. When Sam Smith came out as non-binary, they were mocked by a lot of voices in the mainstream media, which only highlights why it's important these conversations about identity are had more. They are tricky ones to have because people will always have an opinion on topics they don't understand.

My main aim is to open people's minds and help them to understand that there is more out there than just your own personal experiences and existence. We accept that not every single person will follow the same path or believe the same thing, but when it comes to gender and the discussions surrounding it, it becomes a greater problem than it needs to be. We lose the human ability to love and empathise when people like Piers Morgan debate our existence on national television. They aren't doing it fairly. The broadcasters have a certain agenda otherwise they wouldn't create the hysteria.

One particular interview that comes to mind was between the incredibly eloquent Munroe Bergdorf and Piers Morgan. Munroe was debating with an anti-trans campaigner about whether genderfluidity in schools was an issue because 76 children at a certain school in Brighton identified as genderfluid, or said they didn't identify with the gender they were assigned at birth. I agree with what Munroe said at the time: this pushes the battle forward, not backwards. I also understand that conversations around this need to happen for us to move forward as a collective consciousness; however, I'm unsure as to whether doing it on national television does the cause any good. Gender nonconforming and trans people become a mockery, rather than being able to speak for ourselves.

Another tactic the media use is divide and rule: they always use pliable people from minorities that will be mouthpieces for the agenda; they are wheeled out to spurt a bit of controversy surrounding other LGBTQ+ issues before being forgotten about until they need the minority voice again to agree with their side of the debate.

Safe spaces are incredibly important for people in the community to feel accepted. Ginny Lemon and I being able to have *that* discussion on a national TV show sparked a discussion and resonated with a generation that didn't quite get it. I never thought that would be the case but it happened. What made that moment so magical? It was real. It was raw. It was authentic. It was human and it was not a debate. One of the things that brought me most joy after the episode aired were the articles about young people who had seen the conversation between me and Ginny and said it gave them the confidence to come out as non-binary to their mates or their families and have an open conversation about living outside the gender binary. If nothing else, I think my whole time on the show was worth it for that alone.

Trans people exist. Gender nonconforming people exist. Over the years, as we evolve as a species, more and more genders, sexualities and identities are likely to exist and I'm ready to accept these with open arms. Rather than pointing fingers we need to turn it back at the media and stand up for these people.

Our community – the LGBTQ+ community and our allies – isn't getting off lightly over here. I'm grateful that I've been around people that have taught me so much about inclusivity and intentionality, and how discrimination happens everywhere, even when we may not realise it. For example, have you ever thought about whether your local gay venue is accessible to disabled people? Just because we belong to a queer community doesn't mean we're light years ahead of the rest of the world. We still have to work together to challenge discrimination among ourselves and in our own spaces.

Then there's the divide over trans people in some parts of the community. We're never going to get anywhere until trans people and cis women come together. We've seen the rise of the 'gender critical' or trans-exclusionary feminist happening over the years; often they have a number of reasons for their exclusionary views, but one I hear most often is the criticism that a person who decides to transition is playing into gender stereotypes and they should instead remain in their assigned gender to challenge gender roles, rather than transition to feel more comfortable. The thing is, though, that a trans woman is typically a person who feels more comfortable and happier living as a woman – some people might think it's more radical for her to stay living as a gender nonconforming 'boy' or 'man' but that's not how she feels. Personally I think people being able to live happier or more fulfilled lives is more important than having to convince people who think trans people are embracing stereotypes. Some will but plenty of trans and gender nonconforming people defy stereotypes every day.

I'm very airy-fairy sometimes. But when we talk about gender being a spectrum or a social construction (something we as humans invented in order to make sense of the world rather than something innate), I am not trying to undermine a bodily element to the human experience. Myself, many of my cis-female pals and the most famous queer theorist in the world, the American philosopher Judith Butler, would all argue against any kind of feminism that excludes or polices the lives of anyone who is transgender because we all believe that gender is a social construct. Money is also a social construct – doesn't mean you won't go hungry without it. The fact that gender is a social construct doesn't mean that some people don't feel much happier after changing their body by medically transitioning.

Butler says, 'It is always brave to insist on undergoing transformations that feel necessary and right even when there are so many obstructions to doing so, including people and institutions who seek to pathologize or criminalize such important acts of self-definition. I know that for some it feels less brave than necessary, but we all have to defend those necessities that allow us to live and breathe in the way that feels right to us. Surgical intervention can be precisely what a trans person needs – it is also not always what a trans person needs. Either way, one should be free to determine the course of one's gendered life.'

As I keep repeating: the only way forward is everybody coming together. Politically, we're being divided, whether it's race, class, sex, gender; it's all a political agenda to keep people in their own lanes. We need to stand up against this. Straight people need to be true allies and fight homophobia with gay people, instead of just coming to Pride for one weekend a year, enjoying the freedom

of being able to dress up in ways they never normally would, taking advantage of the inclusive environment and then going back to their daily lives (women, queers – hell, ANYONE should be allowed to dress however they please, whenever they please!). I've quite often had straight and cis female friends come to gay bars with me because they don't get harassed. Not wanting to point fingers again, but isn't that a result of the patriarchy?

Then there's racism in the queer community. As a white queer person, I've seen the line-ups. I've seen the club nights. I've seen the lack of diversity and how it's affected my friends who are people of colour. They're exhausted by the constant battle for approval. It's something I know myself and a lot of other white queer people can and should do better on. If we are white, we need to stand up and challenge the racial inequalities within our own community. To create a safe space to challenge the higher cis-tem, our own community must be inclusive and welcoming of everybody. Then we can take over the world, basically.

I remember when Brexit happened (wish I didn't but I do). I was actually in India at the time studying at a yoga retreat. I was with one other British girl and the rest of the people on the retreat with me were from all over the world. I'm lucky to have travelled quite a lot and met so many different cultures and always felt embraced by them all. When the result came in I was mortified. I remember everyone on the retreat being like, 'What the fuck has just happened?' The European Union was essentially brought about by the biggest peace treaty that had ever existed in Western history and we had just gone and left it? I was devastated. I took my anger to a place where we should all direct our anger. Facebook.

I remember writing a status about how the version of the UK I had surrounded myself with was diverse, compassionate and accepting. I gushed about how I felt I had the freedom in London to be myself and that this wasn't the version of Britain I lived in. It wasn't long until a friend of mine who is Black and who experienced life differently to me wrote a comment underneath disagreeing with everything I'd written and spoke about the disproportionate inequality they have ALWAYS faced in Britain. They reminded me of our colonial past (a lot of that colonial past is the reason for a lot of the binary gender reinforcement we have today, of course).

I was 21 at the time. It was a hard pill to swallow. I remember reading it over and over and thinking how blind I had been. Of course Great Britain wasn't so Great. Then I would think about my friends of colour growing up and the micro-aggressions they experienced. I'm sure I would have been part of that problem. I know full well I'm not exempt. That reply on my post widened my horizons to a bigger problem we're facing that goes beyond my own experience and it changed my perspective forever. More voices are speaking up against systemic racism and what they've experienced, but it doesn't stop there. The cis-tem isn't built to benefit the majority, rather a small, elite minority.

I think when it comes to doing your bit, do the most you can and always go into everything with true, authentic intentions. Listen, I'm not telling you to become an activist. Being an ally and activist can occur simultaneously, sometimes dipping between the two as they run parallel. We live in an age where everything is instantaneous. We can find out what's happening on the news as it happens from a smartphone in our pocket. We can also compare ourselves to thousands of images as we aimlessly scroll through our phones. Our attention span has become so short that we have become exhausted. When you're scrolling and you see a petition that might benefit a marginalised group, take the time to sign and share that petition. Internet activism gets a lot of stick because of the speed in which social media is shared, but it can help raise awareness and even make differences to laws.

Quite often an activist group will compose a letter that highlights things that are happening and you can then sign it and send on to your MP. When the Gender Recognition Act (GRA) was being discussed, lots of trans charities and organisations did just that and we fired letters to every MP across the country. If you are ever in the position to donate, even the smallest amount can help non-profit organisations fight for further change. It's about making small steps to lift up the people dedicating their lives to the cause.

There are many forms of activism. I remember taking part in 'Beautiful Radical Activism with Dan Glass'. Dan is a brilliant queer activist in London and held a workshop where I met a group of activists across the field. The workshop was to share ideas on how we would protest certain issues. This one was particularly radical, and I'm not saying you should always seek out the most radical workshops to participate in, but we wouldn't have HIV+ medication if it wasn't for the steps taken by ACT UP, so radical activism has its place!

The importance of activism is about working with people and connecting skills with others to figure out plans to smash the cis-tem. It's crucial to want to work with others; trust me, I've been part of groups that have been incredibly difficult to navigate because a lot of the time people are incredibly passionate and stubborn with their ideals. Seeking out local activism workshops, meetings and groups that ignite a fire in our soul is important and a great way to meet others. I've met many friends from various protests, groups and demonstrations over the years that I've stayed connected with. It's always inspiring to see the chaos they're causing.

Being kind to people in your own life is also incredibly important. Even when I'm not feeling my best I always try to paint a big old, gap-toothed smile across my face, because kindness to strangers costs nothing and gives you that little fuzzy feeling inside. When you think about how time-consuming social media is, how we're juggling trying to live, work, love, be social and have fun all while being crushed by a patriarchal cis-tem that doesn't benefit us, surrounding ourselves with friends that have our backs (and vice versa) during tough times is super-crucial for our own sanity.

People often look at me and say they admire my confidence, but it's not always been there, and quite often still isn't there. But what I do have is a great support network of friends that allow me to be myself and check me if I'm getting out of hand. That kind of love is the most important kind and it's that community we all deserve to find.

Lastly, not taking yourself too seriously is incredibly important for your own peace and happiness. You can be passionate about what you want to achieve and also be proud of any work you create, but the best art comes from fucking up. We learn through our mistakes. One of the most important, and best, skills I ever learned was to laugh at myself. I remember the first few times going on stage looking like an absolute arse-end of a bacon butty and not enjoying one second of it. The energy I was transmitting was feeding into the audience and they could all tell I wasn't enjoying myself. Now, if I perform an act and I slip and fall on my arse I can laugh it off and the audience laughs with me. If I fuck up on set or if a plan didn't go to absolute perfection, that's okay. It's important to remember we're only human and striving to be perfect isn't going to serve anybody.

Quite often when these televised 'debates' happen, our emotion is mistaken for being a 'snowflake'. I say let's avalanche the cis-tem and dismantle the patriarchy. By not taking ourselves seriously it actually allows others to respect and take us more seriously. It might sound weird but it's so true. The minute people sense anguish, they win. Being able to laugh it off is the most powerful tool we can teach ourselves. I implore you at your next Christmas dinner debate, instead of getting angry, just laugh. It'll anger your family member more to see that you don't care whether they agree with you or not. Trust me, it works!

Whenever I've been questioned about my gender nonconformity I always just say, 'You ain't lived a day in my 10-inch thigh-highs and until you have then you can't tell me SHIT'. It pisses them right off. Next time any gender nonconforming or trans person is taken up for a debate we've got to stay calm, cool and collected and let the anger come from the cis-tem we're about to bring down.

Life Lesson 3:
Know Your Her-Story

One of the first trans people to discuss their identity as being neither a man nor a woman was Kate Bornstein, who in their groundbreaking 1994 book *Gender Outlaw* wrote, 'all the categories of transgender find a common ground in that they each break one or more of the rules of gender: what we have in common is that we are gender outlaws, every one of us'. Bornstein is a pretty amazing person with an incredible life story. Assigned male at birth, they grew up uncomfortable with being a boy but fell into the Church of Scientology for several years before leaving, coming out as a trans woman and having sex reassignment surgery. A few months after surgery, though, they realised they weren't a woman either. Kate decided that they would rather define themselves by what they are not – not a man, not a woman. Their book was the first major text to talk about this idea and laid the groundwork for the modern understanding of non-binary identities. Bornstein wrote:

> The first question we usually ask new parents is: 'Is it a boy or a girl?'
>
> There is a great answer to that one going around: 'We don't know; it hasn't told us yet.' Personally, I think

no question containing 'either/or' deserves a serious answer, and that includes the question of gender.

Genderqueer, an earlier term sometimes synonymous with non-binary, was a term first coined in an essay published in the first issue of *In Your Face* (a zine newsletter of the brilliantly named direct action organisation Transsexual Menace) by Riki Anne Wilchins in 1995 to describe anyone who was gender nonconforming. Its use was popularised by the internet and as with all language, its definition has evolved over time. While the term is still relatively new, it's important to know that the history of non-binary genders is expansive and rich in all its gender fuckery and glory!

I had heard of the terms genderqueer and gender nonconforming and always knew that they resonated with my identity. I felt fluid but I was a product of rigid social conditioning, which meant that when I worked in River Island at sixteen they stuck me in the men's department, when all I really wanted to do was look at the fake leather studded jackets upstairs and pretend I was a member of Girls Aloud.

After hearing the term 'non-binary' being used more frequently within my inner social circle in East London and understanding it better, a light-bulb moment happened and the expression made complete sense for my own identity. While the term may be fairly new in mainstream culture, the idea of being outside of the gender binary is actually incredibly old-school and the description of gender nonconforming people has been discussed in loads more places than just *Drag Race UK* and in front of Piers Morgan's oversized ego.

Watching episode three of *Drag Race* was quite difficult in parts as I think it was the first time my family saw me openly discuss my gender identity. I'd always briefly explained that I felt like neither a man or a woman, and that I used drag as a tool to explain the parallels, but I had never been completely honest because I think I was still unsure of myself. It's really important to take the pressure off when figuring out your identity. Even the most accepting, well-intentioned people can expect us to know exactly what we are and what language we want to use to describe ourselves. But in a world where anything but a binary, straight identity is something you have to work out for your self this shit can be confusing. It's different for everyone and being kind to yourself when confused is crucial. You don't have to have all the answers right away. Patience is, as they say, a virtue.

I was unsure as to how *Drag Race* viewers would react to my conversation with Ginny Lemon about non-binary identity, particularly considering how badly some mainstream discussions on the subject have gone in the UK. The topic rarely gets any sensitive or thoughtful coverage, instead it is dismissed or mocked, like the interview with Fox and Owl Fisher, a non-binary couple who are both campaigners and film-makers, on *Good Morning Britain* back in 2017, where Piers Morgan compared identifying as non-binary to identifying as an elephant. I remember distinctly coming to terms with my own gender identity

around this time and seeing the harsh reactions to this conversation from the ever so gracious public on Twitter. Seeing how many people simply disagreed with the existence of non-binary people wasn't exactly encouraging.

The reaction to mine and Ginny's story, fortunately for the two of us, didn't go the same way as it did for Fox and Owl. I was bombarded with messages from people from all walks of life saying that my explanation clicked with them and they understood, for the first time, what it meant to be non-binary. I can't quite begin to explain how overwhelming (in the best way possible) that was. I've always thought if I can change one person's mind then I've done a good job, so to see so many people openly start discussing their own identities, be inspired to come out, and to receive messages from younger audiences saying their parents understood it for the first time, still to this day makes me emotional if I think about it too deeply.

An entire history of gender nonconformity exists, one that isn't covered in our school history lessons because it doesn't fit the Western ideology we've been fed. But it's bigger than gender: I remember being taught that Britain was this great imperial power and that colonisation of other nations during the years of the British Empire was a good thing. How fucked up is that?

This is why discovering and knowing our collective her-story is so important. One of the main ways that the gender binary is reinforced is by pretending that non-binary and gender nonconforming people are new and a fad. It's interesting because while many people

can get their head around someone transitioning from one binary gender to another and even accept that this is a real thing, they cannot accept the idea that the binary itself is an invention and doesn't suit a large number of people. For some, trans men and trans women are valid but non-binary identities are not. This is a shame because it's ignoring the huge shift that is happening in the way many people are thinking about gender. In fact, non-binary people are a larger group among younger people than trans men or trans women: according to a UK Government LGBT survey carried out in 2018, 13 per cent of the respondents were transgender (or trans). Of the total sample, 6.9 per cent of respondents were non-binary (i.e. they identified as having a gender that was neither exclusively that of a man nor a woman), 3.5 per cent were trans women and 2.9 per cent were trans men.

I want everyone reading this to know that how you identify is not up for debate. My motto in life is you can be whoever you want to be as long as you're not harming others. That's my mantra, my daily reminder when I'm getting wound up at little things. One thing is for certain, I ain't going anywhere. I'll be there to remind others and uplift the voices of the marginalised as much as I can until I no longer have a platform. We will not allow the patriarchy to erase gender nonconforming people. To erase history is one of the key ways to deny people their rights. George Orwell (another Penguin author, but with slightly less glamorous cover designs) said: 'The most effective way to destroy people is to deny and obliterate their own understanding of their history.'

On social media, if you're a queer person and you don't know much about LGBTQ+ history then you are sometimes made to feel like a bad person by other queer people who have been busy taking notes from Wikipedia articles. I disagree with that sentiment and think it's wrong to ever shame or ostracise someone for this. We don't know our history because we were never bloody taught it! I could tell you which straight bloke invented the light bulb but I couldn't have told you how the Stonewall riots started, or even what they were about. It's a lot easier now as archives have opened and more LGBTQ+ focused documentaries are coming out, but schools still don't cover any formal LGBTQ+ history.

(I think history should be split into categories that you can choose from at GCSE level on what you would like to learn about.) The conversation surrounding our history is important and shouldn't be dismissed but we all learn in different ways and I think if you're trying to get to grips with some history as an adult you don't have to (just) attend exhibitions or crack books. There are plenty of key moments of queer history you can learn about via television or film. In fact, I'm going to give you some initial recommendations right now.

Bimini's Top Queer Cinema and Television Recommendations

BPM (2017)

Set at the start of the 1990s, this incredible movie follows a group of activists in Paris fighting against the government for its slow efforts to battle the HIV/AIDS epidemic. It mixes energy and emotion and as a queer person reminded me how our lives have always been seen as secondary to those of heterosexuals and how the media made us something to be feared (and still do!). The movie focuses on the incredible work by ACT UP, as well as the personal stories of those fighting for their lives, reflecting on a dark time that affected millions worldwide ... and still does even to this day. It's a total must-watch for everyone, including those that may not quite understand the epidemic. Also, let me remind you that due to activists and scientists we have progressed so far now that someone living with HIV who is on effective treatment can expect to lead a long and healthy life; they also CANNOT pass on the virus. Having an undetectable viral load after

treatment means you cannot transmit the virus. Undetectable = non transmissible. Got it?

Hedwig and the Angry Inch (2001)

This is a fab cult musical focusing on Hedwig, an 'internationally ignored' transgender rockstar. I don't like musicals that much but this one is special. Maybe it's because the styling is that mix of punk grunge and glamour that I adore – and it works. It focuses on her search for stardom and love but also tackles themes of prejudice and discrimination.

Paris Is Burning (1990)

I implore anyone that hasn't watched this to go and watch it now. Put this book down and find a way to watch this film because it is EDUCATIONAL on ballroom culture. I hadn't watched it before I watched *Drag Race* and I was gooped at all the references from this film that are incorporated into the show. What is so magical about *Paris Is Burning* is that it brings you glamour, drama, tragedy and real life. It really is a class of its own. See also Ryan Murphy's *Pose*, a dramatisation of New York's ballroom scenes from the same era.

Buffy the Vampire Slayer (1998–2003)

No, but seriously. You might not think of this show as 'LGBTQ+' but it is one of the queerest mainstream TV series I can think of. Both literally – Willow and Tara's first on-screen kiss in 2001 was one of the very few lesbian displays of affection to air on US mainstream television at that time, and the first on any show with a significant teen audience – and in the subtext. Buffy and Faith's shared dreams, Evil Vampire Willow flirting with her own doppelganger, Buffy 'coming out' as a Vampire Slayer to her mum, Buffy 'penetrating' Angel with a sword to send him to hell and save the world. Must I go on? Angel was responsible for my sexual awakening, by the way.

Death Becomes Her (1992)

Alright, alright, this one might seem like a reach as it is a film all about ostensibly heterosexual women, played by Meryl Streep and Goldie Hawn. However, it is queer because it's Bimini Bon Boulash's favourite film of ALL

TIME and because Meryl and Goldie's characters – two bitter rivals who seek to defy the laws of nature and instead gain eternal youth and beauty in order to pursue the other's total destruction – are basically bloody drag queens. It might not be the best guide to queer history, admittedly, but it is one of the most deliciously camp cult films and has influenced a huge amount of drag culture, including my own drag. 'NOW a warning?'

In the mysterious and mythical world of our mother Earth's ancient history, long before the capitalist abuse of power took over the planet, gender nonconforming humans existed and thrived. In some cultures, gender nonconforming people were gifted magical powers and were looked upon for healing and advice – according to the Greek Anthology (a collection of ancient poems), gender nonconforming priests of the goddess Cybele were so powerful they were able to use magic to make hungry wild lions stop in their tracks instead of feasting on human flesh. Somewhere, J. K. Rowling is trembling in fury at the thought.

The rigid accepted gender binary we see before us

today is a Western, or European, idea of gender imposed on the rest of the world by colonialism. Way before entire continents were plagued by European settlers, gender expression existed outside of the Western binary for thousands of years. Third gender cultures existed around the world and some of them still do today. In Indian culture, Hijras are a third gender role that is neither male nor female. Before the British invasion of India, to be 'homosexual' (or queer) was not illegal until Britain enforced its own sodomy laws on the colonised population, which then criminalised queer people. Not only that, they also criminalised any gender nonconforming people and would make those not wearing correctly gendered clothing strip down and sell their clothes.

Similarly, when North America was colonised, Indigenous 'men' had to cut their braids and 'women' were made to wear dresses. The Western, white gender binary was imposed on Indigenous people, who up until then were accepting of and embraced the full diversity and fluidity of gender. The different cultures in North America had varying attitudes towards sex and gender, and although the modern adoption of the phrase of 'two-spirit' as an umbrella term was created to help English speaking people understand this diversity, not all of them perceived gender in the same way.

Gender nonconforming people were always right here in the UK too. We're very used to seeing depictions in the media of high society throughout the Georgian and Victorian periods, with camp clothes and costumes because they were all extra as fuck back then. I binged

Bridgerton during lockdown like everyone else. But it follows a very heteronormative storyline and we don't hear much about the queers, especially those from the working class. Around the seventeenth century, moral attitudes began to shift, led mainly by a religious movement named the 'reformation of manners', which cracked down on pastimes thought to be frivolous or debauched. Those driving the reformation of manners made it their duty to get rid of any immoral or profane act they viewed as a perversion, especially in the working-class communities. They had a particular fetish for eradicating Mollys, which was a term for effeminate men and a derogatory word for a bloke that had sex with men . . . now I understand why I've had so many straight men try it on with me after MDMA . . .

Those that would now identify in the LGBTQ+ spectrum would all meet in these places called Molly houses (basically, they were like The Glory in East London before The Glory). A lot of them would dress up in drag and many were also prostitutes (the term sex workers is, of course, more appropriate these days). Princess Seraphina, a Molly who is known to history for taking a man to court for stealing her clothes in 1732, is known to be one of the first recognisable drag queens in English history. Everyone called them 'Princess' and they went about most of their day living in women's clothing. On special nights called 'festival nights' a lot of the people in Molly houses would dress in drag and sing, dance and engage in camp behaviour – again this sounds very familiar . . . In the eighteenth century the gradual evolution of modern policing meant that Molly houses were often hassled by officers who would arrest the Mollys for 'misbehaving themselves'. As now, though, gender nonconforming people were punk and often refused to come along quietly, putting up a show of resistance when law enforcement tried to manhandle them.

Gender nonconforming people resisting police harassment leads us nicely into the modern history of the Stonewall riots. Widely recognised as the biggest moment in LGBTQ+ history to date, the Stonewall riots (sometimes called the Stonewall Uprising) took place in New York City and began in the early hours of June 28 1969 at the Stonewall Inn in Greenwich Village as a resistance to police brutality against its queer customers. The history of the riots is more accessible now and more people have told their story. The movement sparked a Western revolution in the journey of rights for queer people, although quite often the involvement of butch lesbians and trans and gender nonconforming people of colour is disregarded, when they actually played a huge role in the act of resistance and in those first years of grassroots activism that emerged after the initial uprising. Sylvia Rivera, Marsha P. Johnson and Stormé DeLarverie are three people whose names have thankfully become more prominent in recent years as queer and gender nonconforming people of colour who were at the heart of the story. Sylvia and Marsha were 'street queens', i.e. drag queens and sex workers who were assigned male at birth but were gender nonconforming and typically used female pronouns. Stormé was a butch dyke, drag king and bouncer.

There are a few different ideas about who started the riots at the Stonewall Inn. Some people say Marsha threw the first shot glass at the mirror behind the bar, which smashed and started the fightback in the community. Some people say Marsha didn't arrive until after the riots started. Others said the first fight with the police happened when Stormé threw the first punch. Whichever story is true, it's thanks to the trans and gender nonconforming people that stood up for the entire community and sparked a torch for the slow-burning acceptance of today. The Gay Liberation Front came from the aftermath of that uprising and actually went on to create the world's very first Pride, which took place on the first anniversary of Stonewall on June 28 1970 in New York City . . . without a Topshop float in sight.

However, did this empower the entire community or did it only empower the big G and mayyybeee a little L in the community?

The majority of people at the front of the Stonewall uprising were either drag queens, gender nonconforming people, or trans women of colour. The role played by Black and Latinx trans people during Stonewall should be more widely recognised today. Individuals from these communities are often the most disregarded and ignored when it comes to their rights today, with many experiencing the brunt of discrimination and living way below the poverty line.

There has sadly always been discrimination within the

queer community, particularly in the 1960s. A lot of white gay men would look down on other people, particularly people of colour and also drag queens and trans/gender nonconforming people. Marsha and Sylvia were told not to attend the very first Pride parade because the white gays thought it would be bad for the community's image . . . imagine that in the days of RuPaul when drag is suddenly aspirational! Turns out white cis gay men weren't always screaming 'YAS QUEEN MAMA TONGUE POP OKURRRRR!' like they do now.

Stonewall took place in the context of a wider civil rights movement. It was a moment in history where marginalised groups came together, learned from each other and fought against a common cause (which is what I think we should do with the patriarchy now). The Revolutionary People's Constitutional Convention, an event organised by the Black Panther Party in Philadelphia in 1970, is an example of a moment where activists from feminist and gay liberation movements,

as well as Black Power, all came together to discuss fighting together for common interests – which I think is pretty inspirational.

Having given you a potted history of gender nonconforming people from the ancient world to the swinging sixties I hope I've got you thinking about how the conversation around trans and non-binary identities has got to where it is now and given you food for thought. I thought it might be useful to end by looking to the future and recommending some of my favourite modern-day icons who are pushing us and the discussion even further forward.

Bimini's Top Gender Nonconforming/ Non-Binary Babes

Yungblud

A musical artist who has received critical acclaim, an allegiance of fans and is known for their punk attitude and fashion sense, Yungblud recently came out as somebody who views gender and sexuality as fluid. In an interview with *Attitude* magazine, Yungblud said they grew up in Doncaster but moved to London for an opportunity to explore and find themselves. 'That's why I am fucking wearing a dress on stage. We've been brought up with such boundaries: woman wears dress, man sees woman's curves, you can make baby.' Someone so public pushing the idea of the deconstruction of gender stereotypes is a modern-day icon in my eyes.

ALOK

ALOK is a badass, internationally acclaimed gender nonconforming performer, speaker and writer. Every time I hear them speak I learn. They are the author of Femme in Public and *Beyond the Gender Binary*. The way they use their wit and intellect to open up tricky subjects surrounding gender and the binary is mind-blowing. It's always inspiring as a non-binary person to hear another person openly talk about how you're feeling. It's important to always be listening to others and ALOK is a person that I could listen to for hours.

ALOK
VAID-
MENON

Travis Alabanza

A human who I'm lucky enough to know personally, and someone I have huge admiration and respect for is Travis Alabanza, an award-winning writer, performer and activist. Their work surrounding gender, trans identity and race has been internationally noted, giving talks at some major institutions such as Harvard and Oxford. Travis is someone that has faced much adversity in the face of staying true to themselves but continues to push the boundaries, being listed by the *Evening Standard* as one of the 25 most influential under 25-year-olds. A huge feat for a non-binary icon!

Jonathan Van Ness

Jonathan Van Ness is an uber babe. I fell in love with them on the reboot of *Queer Eye* and I am still in awe at their spirit. I've never met them but they project through the screen as a human that would light up a room and make everyone laugh. Jonathan uses their charm and sass to make people feel comfortable enough to open up and talk about their experiences and they use their platform to do the same. They have a podcast called *Getting Curious* with Jonathan Van Ness where they tackle everything from colonisation to oppression and I always adore hearing another non-binary point of view in the mainstream.

Meg-John Barker

Meg-John Barker has penned various books ranging from gender to sexuality and breaks down complex information into digestible chunks for everyone to read. I got papped in Norwich buying one of their books from a small book shop actually . . .

Jamie Windust

Jamie Windust. The icon themselves. They are an LGBTQ+ activist, model, writer and speaker and also have a bloody great sense of style and self. They write regularly for cool publications like *Dazed*. I've followed Jamie for many moons now and I adore their use of bright colours and mixed prints. It's always daring and it always works. I love a person that isn't afraid to get down and dirty with a mixed print. They're such a huge advocate for representation and they're also another one of those intelligent people I love to read or listen to because they have the language that helped my non-binary booty get a bit more of an understanding of my own self.

Life Lesson 4:
Where Are the Bitcheees?

Are you a boy or a girl? Or what?

When I was 18 I moved to London from the small seaside town of Great Yarmouth to study fashion journalism. As I've already said (and if you have eyes you've probably noticed) I have always been a bit of a show-off, so when I arrived in London I wasn't remotely scared of the big city and fast pace of life – I was excited. I turned up at the open day for my first student halls at the University of the Arts London with a fake Louis Vuitton bag, skinny jeans and an oversized denim shirt. I thought I looked the shit and I remember thinking to myself, 'I've arrived! She's in London now.'

Everyone came to the very first party I held in my halls that initial week of university and met each other for the first time, so let's just say I cemented my reputation as a party girl. I actually applied to be an official Freshers' Rep but they turned me down as they thought I was too drunk and disorderly! Who really needs to be an official rep when you're out on the town every single night (which I was for the entire first month I was in London)? It wasn't long before I discovered the city's queer scene, with its two main hubs, Soho and East London.

It was at this time that I also first encountered London's drag scene. Back then, there was one queen who reigned supreme: hostess, DJ, music producer and promoter Jodie Harsh. Jodie is a dear friend now so I say this with love and respect but the first few times we met she was an actual wanker to me (love ya babe). I can remember being at one of her parties and reaching to pour myself a vodka from a bottle that was on the table and she slapped my wrist, took the bottle and snapped, 'I pour the vodka around here'. While I was stunned at the rudeness, I have to say I also found it incredibly iconic. She really was the 'it girl', long before drag had the huge renaissance it's had in London over the past few years.

The explosion in popularity and evolution of London's drag scene was driven largely by a new party called Sink The Pink, which was founded by Glyn Fussell and Amy Zing, two friends from Bristol, in 2008. Sink The Pink began in an old working men's club in Bethnal Green and has grown into one of the most famous queer parties in the world. I remember looking at Sink The Pink back when I first started going out and thinking it was the coolest thing ever. These people did not give a fuck what they were wearing; they were all dressing up in bright colours and I felt completely in awe. You have to remember that at this time I was not 'seriously' doing drag. I was hanging out with people who were, though. People like Fifi la True (the drag persona of Jamie Campbell, who inspired the hit musical *Everybody's Talking About Jamie*).

I remember very occasionally experimenting with drag early on, at around the age of 20, by arriving at club nights in a fur coat and just underwear (to be honest, I do the exact same thing now but on the covers of fashion magazines, darling). I can remember the first time I went out in a slip dress and a long blonde wig and a friend had done my makeup. I felt like the most gorgeous, femme thing in the room: you could not have told me any different. Of course, it helped that at that time the club photographers used to airbrush the hell out of all the photos so I could maintain my delusions of grandeur. However, some of the actual drag queens were quick to throw some shade my way. I can remember a few of the bigger name queens I knew on the scene back then telling me that what I was doing wasn't real drag and to be honest it was intimidating. Even though at that time I didn't have the confidence to do drag 'properly' I was still watching and learning more about it from the side lines, while rocking a 1980s Club Kid aesthetic. To give you an idea: I had orange hair and dyed my eyebrows blue. I may have been nervous to fully

throw myself into doing drag in my early days but I guess slow and steady won the race, because here I am years later writing a drag queen's guide to life. Ha!

Looking back on this time in my life, it's obvious that I was searching for myself and for my community. I think everyone does this to a certain extent when they're young, but for queer people it's absolutely crucial because we often grow up hiding parts of ourselves at school, or live in parts of the country where there are fewer queer people and so we are isolated. This means we have fewer opportunities to meet others like ourselves and create those spaces where it's safe to experiment with how we look, what we do, how we dress and what we call ourselves – without shame or judgement. Often, it's the big cities like London or Manchester or the famously queerer towns like Brighton that become hubs for this sort of identity exploration. The importance of 'chosen family' among LGBTQ+ people is something that cannot be overstated. It's introduced well in the film *Paris Is Burning* (which I recommended in the last chapter). At the very end of the movie, two young, effeminate boys who

have run away from families that didn't accept them have ended up in the Harlem queer community around the ballroom scene and one of them explains how the people in their community form family ties with each other to replace the families they lost when they came out: 'They treat each other like sisters, or brothers, or mothers. You know like I say, "That's my sista", because she's gay too and I'm gay.'

Luckily, not every gay, queer or trans person will go through the extreme experience of family rejection seen in this movie. However, many LGBTQ+ people will have gone through a process of trying to find a safe space and a sense of community; they'll have felt a similar sense of belonging and acceptance when they first stepped on to a queer scene and found their sisters, siblings or queer family. This is why queer spaces and nightlife venues are so important. I can't help wondering what it would have been like for me if I'd moved to London during a pandemic when all nightlife had completely stopped. So many young people coming of age over the past couple of years will have had this experience. Imagine not being able to go out and dance in a sweaty club to 'Chromatica' by Lady Gaga, dressed like god knows what, making best friends with people you only started chatting to five minutes ago in the smoking area?

Personally, I think experiencing this is important for so many young queer and trans people who are discovering who they are. That's why we all need to fight for our queer spaces and independent venues, which have taken a real financial bashing during this time. It's not like they weren't struggling before the pandemic either – for years greedy property magnates have been buying up urban spaces, pushing up rents and turning illustrious LGBTQ+ venues into luxury flats almost no one can afford. As things start to open back up again, I plan to go to the independent queer venues in London that need financial support as much as possible – for me, that's places like The Glory and Dalston Superstore, but I encourage everyone reading this to get out there and to support their local LGBTQ+ venues and spaces, no matter where you live or what form they take.

'I used to dance at Savage Discos, now they're luxury flats!' is a lyric from one of the songs I've recorded called 'Ain't it Wonderful'. It's about life in London and how

you can take away our dance floors but we'll never go away. At its core, it explores what hedonism is all about. Queer spaces are crucial for our well being (most of the time) but everywhere has a price. Nightlife is disposable to people earning the big bucks but they can never get rid of us. We're like me in 2015 at an after-party . . . going nowhere.

I've been to pretty much every queer club in London and a lot of straight ones too. I spent the majority of my early twenties off my face on a dance floor. I had some of the best nights of my life and met people that I went on to be friends with forever. I explored who I was, my sexuality and experienced a sense of freedom I had never tasted before. It wasn't always sunshine but it sure felt like it. Nothing beats that feeling of looking around a sweaty dance floor and seeing your mates who GET IT, who GET YOU . . . it does wonders for the soul. It's like medicine. I wish I had millions of pounds so I could buy every queer venue and keep it there forever. They are as culturally important as museums and parks. They can't keep receding into nothingness like my hair-line. They need to stay. Like my hairline does too (honestly, the levels of gender dysphoria I feel).

It's important to mention that even though this kind of queer nightlife and scene were incredibly formative for me, and helped me to discover queer community and a chosen family in London, there are many other fun ways to engage with London's queer community, find fellow queers and gain that all-important sense of community and belonging. There are so many reasons why queer people might not feel entirely comfortable going into these kind of alcohol and drug-centred spaces – that's perfectly okay and it's never your place to question anyone on this! We already know that higher levels of substance abuse exist within the LGBTQ+ community and it's pretty alienating for people to realise that a high number of queer events that they might be interested in involve alcohol in some capacity. Queer people don't exactly need to be marginalised any further than they already are, especially in their own spaces. The problem is, with venue closures, there's already a lack of LGBTQ+ spaces in London generally, so trying to find spaces that aren't alcohol-focused as well is like trying to find a tiny arse needle in a bloody big haystack. It's not happening! I often hear queer people speak out about how they really struggle to navigate the lack of sober safe spaces available to the LGBTQ+ community. We need more options for queer safe spaces that offer both sober and fully accessible events. I love this idea because without a reliance on alcohol sales, they end up being more community-focused, DIY, a big 'fuck you' to capitalism and they ensure that everyone feels safe, welcomed and accepted. A big win I'd say.

So, what are the different routes to finding queer community? There are really cool community spaces like The London LGBTQ+ community centre which is a completely accessible, multi-purpose space run for and by LGBTQ+ people. It's a safe space for the community to hang out, run events, meet people – and it even has a sober hangout café! Recently, a new bookshop/

café has opened in Shoreditch that prioritises queer people of colour, queer women, non-binary people and the trans community. They have a downstairs events space and even a podcast-recording studio. There are also plenty of small community sober raves and club events – take MISERY for example. They are a grass-roots organisation, mental health collective and sober club night centring on healing and joy for queer, trans, non-binary and intersex Black people and people of colour. C.Y.O.A. is another sober LGBTQ+ dance party that happens at DIY Space for London for people who want a night out without alcohol/intoxicants. I'd recommend using Google to find out if there are any events like this near you and I encourage you to get involved and support them if you can. You could even volunteer for a queer-focused charity if there are any near you, this might be a great way to meet like-minded people and find a sense of community. If we support these spaces then hopefully they can continue to thrive and be a life-line for those who need them.

Even though queer nightlife in London helped shape who I am today that doesn't mean it's always been a psychedelic acid trip of live, laugh, love. I used to be a 'live fast, die young' kinda girl. I had that naive, twenty-something-couldn't-tell-me-nothing attitude and I thought I had life figured out. I always believed myself to be naturally headstrong – which is true still – but when it came to partying and drugs . . . I smashed it. I was always the last one standing, although often that was because I didn't sleep. I never admitted it to myself at the time because I thought I was just young and having fun but I had developed a problem with drug use.

I had experienced a lot of heartache leading up to my early twenties. Navigating the world as a queer person, experiencing a lot of mental abuse, losing my best friend in a freak accident that shook our entire town. Even the most optimistic person would have taken a punch. I was always up for a party but that desire became worse without realising how all those incidents in my life had affected me. I found myself in situations I never could have imagined, with people I didn't really know, doing things I shouldn't. I was very lonely even though I was surrounded by people for days on end. The occasional drug became more regular and at this period in my life I became reliant on substance abuse. Even though I was always a weed smoker, drugs didn't have a significant hindrance in my daily life; it wasn't until I started taking GHB that things became a lot darker.

GHB. Satan in liquid form. But sadly, the best feeling of euphoria I have ever experienced. A lot of people use it in a sexual way but I didn't. It made me feel confident. It made me able to project out the person I felt on the inside: all my troubles didn't exist anymore and all the little chips on my soul vanished. It's worse than cocaine in how it made me act (like a wanker) but I didn't realise. I was oblivious. I was delusional under drugs. I got so caught up in the hedonism of London that I think I would have died. If I had continued down that path I wouldn't be here now. It was no longer fun and I became a version of myself I despised. It knocked my confidence and I've had to work really hard on my mental health over the years (and I still do . . . it hasn't been magically cured) through lots of different routes, some of them cliché. I had my Madonna 'Ray of Light' era after the drugs and I wouldn't have it any other way . . . except maybe less psytrance.

I'm not alone in this. In the 2017 national survey on drug use and health they reported that those who identify as gay or lesbian are twice as likely as those who identify as heterosexual to develop substance abuse issues. Those that are unsure of their identity, whether that's sexual or gender, were five times as likely to have a substance-use disorder than heterosexual people. That statistic is harrowing but paints an idea about how identity and sexuality can fuck you up. That's why when people argue the existence of people within the LGBTQ+ it's reductive. Do you think we want to feel guilt and shame for not being society's expectation?

In 2016, I moved back to London after time spent travelling in India, finished my degree and began living with my friend Byron and other queer people in a converted warehouse in East London. I had largely fallen out of the queer scenes where drugs and hedonism had

become a major problem for me a couple of years earlier. Now, with this new group around me, I started going to Sink The Pink again and dipped my toe back into that world. I had missed the queer energy and being a part of that scene, but needed both some time away from it and for the dynamics to be right for me to return; my first era on that scene had taken over my physical and mental health and happiness in a way that was detrimental. Everything seemed to fall right this time though and, like Madonna, I reinvented myself.

One of the people I lived with was Barbs, whom I still live with today. Barbs is my drag sister and we went through all the chaos of navigating the drag scene and becoming the (delusional) stars we are today together. We've been with each other since the very first moment we stepped on stage – actually before that in the grotty warehouse – but we have grown together. I'm thankful to have a friend like Barbs because we take the piss out of each other but also ground each other when one's ego is getting monstrous. She's a nut-bag and an absolute superstar. Long live Barbs, the wrinkly old witch.

During the time in which I had stepped away from the queer scene, drag in London had gone nuclear, thanks to the combined effect of Sink The Pink and the huge popularity and growing mainstream success of *Drag Race*. Venues like The Glory in Haggerston had become focal points for this new explosion and I remember going and seeing people on stage and thinking, 'I can do that, I can lip-sync'. With a supportive community around me, I started to think I had more to offer the queer world so I decided to enter The Glory's drag competition LIPSYNC1000 in February 2017. Bimini Bon Boulash was born. I put on a pink wig and performed a political number where I came out lip-syncing as Hilary Clinton. It ended with me tying 'Donald Trump' (my mate Coleman) to a chair, stripping to the song 'Down in Mexico', stripping 'Trump' to reveal 'MAKE AMERICA GAY AGAIN' written on his chest and giving him a lap dance. It was my first ever performance as Bimini and it got me to the final.

These days, a lot of queens will spend years perfecting their makeup on Instagram before they so much as leave the house but in my first two years doing Bimini I was a MESS. I believe all drag queens should have this period. You should have those times where you're just going out and having fun and looking like shit – I love that there are photos of me out there where I look like a fucking shambles with eyebrows an inch too high and poorly covered stubble. For the first two years doing Bimini, from 2017 to 2019, drag wasn't something I was getting paid for and Barbs and I weren't taken very seriously. No one expected that we would be the queens who proved ourselves and started taking over the big drag competitions. In the same way, years later on *Drag Race UK*, no one saw Bimini coming. It was in late 2018 that I started taking drag more seriously and I got my first paid gig at a night called 'Bender' at The Eagle in Vauxhall, south London. It only lasted three months (I think I was a bit too much of a gender bender for the masc gays that frequented the place) but with the money I got paid every Friday night

for performing I was able to save for my entry to the Miss Sink The Pink 2019 pageant – the biggest drag pageant in East London. After performing a slow and sensual piece to Tina Turner's 'Private Dancer', which included an intricate pole routine with a drop from the top into a split, Bimini Bon Boulash was crowned the winner of the pageant. It was around this time that I went full-time and drag became not just my passion, my community and my family – it also became my job.

Earlier on in this chapter, I spoke about the importance of community spaces and queer nightlife and how we all need to come together to preserve them. Saving these venues is especially important for the drag community because we rely on these spaces for our livelihoods. Before the pandemic hit, the drag scene in London was booming. Everyone was working. There were growing numbers of drag kings. There were more women and non-binary people becoming drag queens. Since the pandemic, the industry has been on its knees because there's been no help or financial assistance from the Tory government, particularly for self-employed people. When *Drag Race* paused filming during the first lockdown it was a huge struggle financially for me (as it was

for many people). Friends of mine had to leave drag to find work so that they could survive. There were moments when I thought maybe I needed to do the same. It was only performing at an outdoor cabaret night called Touché at The Cause that saved me in the summer of 2020. It gave a lot of queer people jobs but things remained tough. I'll also say grace to the huns, because if it wasn't for them coming to brunches I'd have been out of work and probably back to one of my mediocre side hustles.

Queer spaces and community are so important because they allow us to be authentic versions of ourselves. We arrive at these places like fresh, young, queer vegan eggs (sometimes older queer vegan eggs) and discover that there are people out there just like us who have also experienced hardship and discrimination because of their gender identity, expression or sexuality. When all of us come together under one roof to drink, validate each other and dance the night away it's bloody powerful. I've never experienced fighting or physical violence inside queer spaces, but I have seen heteronormative propaganda, homophobic or transphobic insults and abuse outside of a venue. I have watched how fellow LGBTQ+ people have worked their way around these venues and found themselves. I have witnessed people older than me doing drag and having an entire room under their spell. People like Baga Chipz ruled Soho when I was first thrust upon the nightlife scene, and I watched in awe at the freedom and confidence these people expressed. The significance of these spaces can't be overstated. My boyfriend grew up in a Catholic environment and for him moving to London meant he was finally able to find community and safe spaces to freely express his queer identity. That's what London is about. It draws in dreamers, people who want more than the life that has been given to them.

The fact that drag is more mainstream now has its ups and downs. Like I discussed earlier, it's important that we remember all of the gender nonconforming and trans people who came before us and are the reason why LGBTQ+ rights are where they are today. Not all styles of drag are given an equal footing and quite often members of the drag community are forgotten about entirely. I'm so lucky to have come up through a scene that actively tried to champion diversity and fairness and welcomed everyone to drag with open arms, regardless of identity or what's between your legs. That's how all drag scenes should be and it's important for me to champion this idea and keep it going for the queers to come.

And yet another result of drag becoming mainstream is oversaturation and the dilution of the radical essence of drag as an art form. I love a brunch as much as the next bitch but there is an issue when venues for queer people are closing down all over the place and leaving drag queens on every block twirling around outside an All Bar One. The space that drag takes up should always be punk and authentic and often this doesn't really fit with a Britney-themed brunch – trust me, I've performed at many! These largely heteronormative spaces are purely using drag for entertainment (and rightly so, it's bloody entertaining). However, the struggles that queers go through to find safe spaces, chosen family and

community will never be fully understood by the majority of the straight, cis world. Even the best ally can only empathise. These spaces are a lifeline for us. I'm happy to be put into your music videos and entertain you on a Saturday lunchtime, but don't take the piss and don't see us as a gimmick, love. Drag becoming mainstream doesn't mean it should be absorbed and devoured by straight culture.

When I create shows I want them to be as representative of the world I've come from as possible. Recently, I did 'An Evening with Bimini Bon Boulash', where I invited kings and queens from East London to the stage of Clapham Grand and the Albert Hall in Manchester. I don't take my platform for granted and want to give space to a real group of artists that I've hustled and grinned with over the years. It's that East London family thing again. Local drag is the best kind of drag.

My advice? Go out and support the dolls and the ken dolls. Don't just book to see us RuGirls – go and check out the local talent in the bars near you. By doing so, you'll be helping a venue to stay open and allowing a queen or a king to invest in their art.

Most of us don't start drag to get famous, we start drag because it's a part of us. For me, it was the gateway to exploring my identity. Maybe for others it is about fame – it's a desirable perk, I guess. Take it from me though, brush your teeth before a 6am dog walk because there might be some snap happy people around . . .

To keep this world of drag and performance alive, we all need to come together. If you look at the segregation of Pride events happening across the UK it shows how much separation the community is experiencing right now. Trans Pride is an incredible event that happens across the UK, but it was created in retaliation to trans people feeling side lined by the LGBTQ+ community. So listen: we're stronger together than we are divided; right now there's never been a more important time for us all to unite against the cis-tem and slimy corporations trying to take away our queer spaces and dilute our art. Let's go!

We're in this together or we're not in this at all. For all of those that enjoy queer nightlife we must stand together to protect it. This sounds like some action movie and I'm standing in a really camp flowing cape with my hands on my hips and a proud stance (a bit like I am on the cover). No, seriously, at all costs we must protect because the Torys sure as hell don't care that 50 per cent of London's queer nightlife has closed down since 2010. I have friends who are cishet women that love nothing more than getting pissed in a queer venue because they feel safe. Major red flags in society aside, I believe we can work together to protect these spaces. Go out and support those venues that need it (that's all of them!) and go to nights that are put on by queer people to help the community thrive and reinvigorate after the trauma it's experienced. If you're straight and cishet, remember to have respect when you enter these spaces. That isn't being a wanker; it's being honest. You're welcome in these bars; literally, you're welcome everywhere so please respect and cherish these safe spaces for queer people if you attend them and let's dance to the Spice Girls . . . or some techno beat if we're being cool.

Life Lesson 5:
Suffer for Fashion

When I strutted down that runway on *RuPaul's Drag Race UK* I was feeling every type of fantasy. I served a bacterial, alien-like organism for the 'prehistoric' challenge (you know I love to take a risk!) and felt like the primordial queer cell. I walked my finale runway in a bridal/punk-inspired corset and train that snatched my waist tighter than Jeff Bezos (because all great couture runways end on . . . bridal!). Hell, I even gave you pure nineties British football hooliganism, which you all slept on because of a bit of tape. One day that tape will be part of a V&A exhibition on Bimini's fashion, I promise you. If it isn't, I'll sell it on Craigslist.

Basically what I'm trying to say is I bloody love fashion. It's a spectacular art form – my favourite art form, regardless of whether art snobs say it isn't one. It excites me. I love its transformative process and how you can use it to make a statement, blend in or do something unexpected and outrageous. There are so many reasons why fashion is so important to me and my self-expression as Bimini. So this chapter is all about the wonder of fashion, darling.

Fashion is important for a lot of queer people. I was always secretly obsessed with it but I haven't always been the risk taker I am today. In fact, I've gone through more style evolutions than Madonna – and counting. Some of them have been great and some of them have been truly awful, but what's life without looking like trash for a few years?

Let's go back in time to when I was a wee wane growing up in Norfolk. My mum would dress me as a child, obviously, in plenty of denim and GAP because it was the nineties and my mum was a style icon. 'Like Edina Monsoon' my auntie would joke, but I believe that to be one of the biggest compliments anyone could receive. Who doesn't want to look like Eddie, sweetie?

We know I was always a bit of a flamboyant attention seeker who worked hard to hide the truly camp core of my personality (I was Edmund in my stage school's depiction of *The Lion, The Witch and The Wardrobe* . . . CAMP!). But this flamboyance wasn't evident in my style until I left high school. During those dreaded early teen years I tried to fit in with the lads, which meant I didn't have the courage needed to shred some fishnets and safety-pin an outfit together and say, 'I'm punk, mate'. Instead I wore grey McKenzie tracksuits and those K-Swiss trainers from JD that have the little weird

bit that you can move. A flawed design? Or a detail so trendy it fooled nobody that I was straight? Me and the lads would walk around the town centre dressed in similar tracksuits, but never the same, each grey shade strategically chosen so as to not upset the straight king bee, each McKenzie design splashed across a different part of the hoodie. The lads would banter and I'd try to get involved but sometimes it was just nasty. Why does heteronormative culture encourage that?

In 2006 my high school didn't have much of an alternative scene so I repressed my desire to dress how I wanted to and did everything I could to not upset the status quo; the complete opposite of what I've promised myself I'll do now as an adult.

The psychology of style and fashion is incredibly fascinating to me. Even the way I dressed in my early teens in order to fit in and be like everyone else represents a basic human desire to be liked. When I think about all of my style icons now, they all share a similar unapologetic approach to being themselves, which I've learned comes as you *cue sick bucket* find *yourself*. I wasn't ready to be myself so I happily accepted Lynx Africa and a JJB Sports voucher for Christmas because it was a lot easier than telling everyone that I actually wanted to be in a perfume advert for Britney Spears' 'Fantasy'.

What's funny is how much of a sponge I was for the style I grew up around. I may not have been able to wear a Juicy Couture tracksuit back then but I sure have made up for it now. I guess I looked at everything that was going on during this era in pop culture, suppressed it until I was ready to live it, and here we are. Fourteen years later and I'm one pencil-thin bitch brow away from being a true nineties groovy chick. Fun Fact: *Grazia* recently did a trend article about the revival of the nineties Pamela pencil brow and I was referenced in it as a bitch brow trendsetter. Sorry, people, but a bushy brow is so last year. Get those tweezers out!

I had my first queer real-life experience when I was 14. It wasn't sexual, it was . . . magical. I was stood outside the battered Hollywood cinema in Great Yarmouth, probably having a fag with my best mate who silently knew I was queer but who humoured my confusion about it until I was ready, and there they were in my sight line. A vision in studded tartan and leather, a stylised bleached

mullet with complementary sunglasses and a platform shoe to boot. It may sound like I'm describing my own style . . . but it came from somewhere else.

I had never seen a visibly, unapologetically queer person in the flesh before and behold, here one was right in front of me. Like a true Ray of Light ('never one to pass up a Madonna reference), they shone. To me, anyway. I think to the average person living where I grew up this person would have looked like a weirdo, a freak. But it was the most punk thing I've ever seen and frankly I couldn't work out if I wanted to be them or I wanted to fuck them, a similar feeling I got when I saw Pete Burns on *Celebrity Big Brother*. The likelihood is that it

was probably a bit of both. It was in that moment that I knew one day I was gonna be as authentically *myself* as this person was. I have no memory of what I saw at the cinema that evening, but this person, whoever they were, is etched into my brain whether I like it or not, a bit like U2's album on every iPod Nano in 2010.

It took about 18 months after this encounter before I took my style into my own hands. I remember the shock of buying my first pair of skinny jeans from the 'women's' section and feeling like I'd done something terrible. This pair of black River Island jeans fit more snugly than any straight cut jeans in the land of two for £12. Then there were the awful beige tees, and those weird scarf things that every indie boy wore in 2007, along with that almost pirate-esque bandana print. You know the one I mean. Not only did the jeans fit me in all the right places, they made my butt look phenomenal. With Panic! At the Disco blasting in my ears, my hormones racing and my teen heart beating faster, I was ready to conquer the world ... or at least try and survive two years of the word FAG being hurled at me at least three times a day until I could move to the bright lights of the big city.

Reflecting back and feeling nostalgic, I'm quite proud of myself for experimenting at that age. When I turned 15 I learned that gender and clothing is something we all get to customise for ourselves and that I could mimic rockstars and icons that had deviated from expectations. Sure, the way I actually executed it was really shit and my taste level was questionable, but knowing that charity shops existed was the best thing ever for my young queer self. It taught me that you can get an entire outfit for less than an eighth of weed, which my best friend and I would be delighted at when our mates would be spending all their money earned from part-time jobs on one top from Zara and we could spend the extra on cigarettes and hairspray.

This was a time when I longed to be seen as an individual, not a generic indie kid. As Laura Marling said, 'Where did the indie in individual go?' The trend was Topshop, and Topshop was known for their polka-dot dresses that all the indie kids would wear, becoming the absolute antithesis of the word, but that was the culture in the late 2000s. Folk and indie bands were more popular than ever. Everybody wanted a slice of the Arctic Monkeys or to be wasted at Latitude festival listening to Mumford & Sons. God, I miss being clueless and wearing a tee from a band I'd never listened to.

More importantly, charity shops taught me not to follow trends. We would jeer at photos of celebrities because it seemed nobody was giving a shit about being innovative anymore. Maybe that's why I became so attached to Lady Gaga and her outlandish style. She was fresh and daring. She was making me feel something. It was exciting to watch. She's a fashion icon, not because everything she wore was incredible – because she definitely shot and missed a few times (we all have) – but because she's not afraid to go all the way.

Granted, I've missed many times. My hair was 'off' for years and bright blue, but the fur coats and fishnets I'd skulk around town in looked banging and I would smoke cigarettes and drink Diet Coke and pretend to be Kate Moss with my best mate. We promised to have a baby named Vivienne one day and we put a picture of Patsy Stone at the top of our Christmas tree. We spent Christmas and New Year's Eve at hers once and we smoked so much weed we passed out at 10pm, woke up at 2am having missed the countdown, opened a bottle of Bollinger, had one glass and went back to sleep. Let's just say I'm thankful I'm still a fashion icon and I'm no longer a massive stoner. The bags I carried under my eyes ain't the look.

I've name-dropped some of my many nonconforming fashion icons. (Don't you worry, I'll be delving deeper into that a bit later.) But for now I want to emphasise again how I dressed better than the entire population of Great Yarmouth before they even knew it. Still got called FAG quite a lot though. Actually, scrap that, I *still* get called FAG quite a lot. Fuck it.

Behind those cheap fur coats and ash-covered cans of Diet Coke was my first insight into my own freedom of expression. One of the most important freedoms that we should all be taught at school to respect, both in our-selves and others, is the ability to express yourself freely. They tell us to be unique but then we have to conform to school policy and wear uniforms (even though we all tried to make our uniform look as slutty as possible: my tie was way less than four stripes and actually looked ridiculous). We're still being taught to all follow the same path. School uniforms have a history of rebellion and conformity and whether you loved or loathed having a

school uniform, a lot can be said about its subliminal disregard of individual identity. It stifles expression, but it probably saved me from wearing a lot more Burton jeans, so swings and roundabouts. Bring back the navy cardigan!

Now on to the people who made me an icon. Saying that might sound a bit cocky, but the thing about any icon is that they are the product of a team. Designers, stylists, makeup artists, choreographers. Every diva you love might have had raw talent but she was built up to icon status by a wider collective. When I call myself an 'icon' it's to acknowledge the people around me who made it possible and their talents. Truthfully I am, in a sense, the final product of the hard graft and creative vision of others as much as myself.

As I mentioned in the last chapter, at the start of my drag career I was rather . . . experimental, shall we say. I had an idea of how you were supposed to do drag and what that was supposed to look like. Obviously now I'm of the mindset that there are absolutely zero rules when it comes to drag, because drag is personal to each individual artist who does it. However, I didn't always see

that and before my rebellion I succumbed to conformity. I'm not going to mention the names of the people on the London drag scene that I looked to for inspiration in the early days; quite frankly because I don't think they'd appreciate it. I do remember when I started dabbling with makeup and wigs when I first came to London I was harshly critiqued by a queen in a smoking area of Room Service, one of Jodie Harsh's popular club nights, for not doing drag 'properly'. Unsurprisingly, the look she tore apart was a pair of fishnets and a fur coat (recurring theme) but what I lacked was a confidence to *tongue pop* *sell* the garment, mama. I've never been able to convince myself I'm feeling confident when I'm not. True confidence came later, after gradually exploring who I am and my own identity, which then snowballed into all of the fashion you've seen today. As I got more confident with age, I basically decided to ignore all the rules I had imposed on myself about how I thought drag was supposed to look and do my own thing. Which is great for me because I fucking hate sequins.

Not all artists are lucky enough to have an Ella Lynch in their life. Ella and I met when we worked in a community music venue called Passing Clouds (which sadly fell victim to London's luxury flats fetish) and I was dressing like a hippy, with an array of rainbow-coloured prints – not worn in irony and certainly not around Pride. After my years of hedonism I had fled from London to travel across the globe to find myself at the bottom of a bucket of SangSom. When I returned to London I couldn't bring myself to return to the queer scene immediately because I was scared of losing my way again. That's when I met Ella. Ella worked on costumes at Passing Clouds; when I joined we had such an immediate connection in our shared love of attention-seeking that soon I allowed Ella full creative control over what dragon head or feathery headpiece I would be wearing that evening (much to the staff's dismay). They weren't always our finest fashion hours but it was the start of something magical, a creative partnership that would go on to blow people's minds (maybe I can be delusional after all . . . or perhaps it's just confidence).

Fast-forward to 2018 when Ella moved in with me and our partnership started to step up a gear. Ella is hugely inspiring to me as a visionary artist. She's got one of those eyes for creativity that is really rare. It's referential, it's sexy, it's camp. Ella knows exactly how to add a magic touch to an idea or an outfit to elevate it and give it just that bit extra. I'm grateful to her not only for working with me to push my style and evolve by creating jaw-dropping outfits, but for encouraging my confidence to grow. We both do it for each other. It's a very uplifting relationship in that we allow each other to be as creative as possible. It's a nurturing of both our talents. I welcome the chaos. I encourage the outlandish. I'm up for it, and that pushes Ella even further.

The week Ella moved in I had some red fabric lying around and she draped it on me and styled a look from pieces I had in my room for a queer fashion show. I turned up and felt a million bucks; that night just set off a domino effect of fabulous fashion moments for Bimini. Ella would often style or push my styling further for random club night gigs I had. What's beautiful about it all is that we were doing this when nobody gave a shit. It was always that commitment to the look, that extra level of over-the-top that always had us hungry for more. I would often (and still do) call Ella my Nicola Formichetti (foremost stylist and fashion director to Lady Gaga at the height of her fame, or quite often when I was winding her up I'd call her Mikey, as in Erika Jayne's creative director.

It's never serious, but we take it seriously.

Ella has done a number of iconic looks for me. We invented the colour 'mint green' for my Miss Sink The Pink performance, which I won by gyrating on a pole while my dancers shot money with my face on it at me. She did my Pete Burns tribute look for Pride, where I did a 'reveal' in which I transitioned from eighties Dead or Alive Pete into the Vivienne Westwood-wearing Pete Burns we remember today (god rest your soul Pete, you fucking icon). But I would probably say that, prior to

Drag Race, my all-time favourite Ella Lynch x Bimini moment was when I went to New York City.

Nobody asked for this level of extra but we decided to give it to them anyway. I didn't have a lot of money but I had been in the clubs all summer doing the circuits and hustling. I'd stopped drinking and I was investing pretty much all the money I made back into my drag. I spent a lot of money on this particular look and piecing together the components but it was worth it. It was the birth of Bimini's high-rise leotard and thigh-high combination. Later, Ella and I would reference ourselves and this look again on *Drag Race* (I love that Ella and I reference *ourselves* a lot as well; it's so conceited).

Back to New York. Me and some of the East London queens did a London Takeover at Bushwig Festival in Brooklyn. We loved it. I really pushed myself for the entire trip and people were taking notice. I remember one of my good friends and fellow drag icon Grace Shush saying to me, 'Wow, you're blowing my mind with these looks. You're working so hard!' She said it because I wore a Westwood-inspired tartan minidress with a netted hammock I had fashioned into a cape/shawl moment covered in safety pins. Grace was impressed and I was feeling the moment, but that wasn't even the peak of my New York looks.

My USA cycling look was where I really felt like I was making a fashion statement. Ella spent ages stoning the details on a cycling top she then fashioned into a leotard and paired with some cycling sunglasses and diamanté earrings. (Did you know diamanté means fake diamond?

Love that.) Anyway, me and some of my drag sisters went to Susanne Bartsch's night On Top with Amanda Lepore – a massive icon – and people's heads were turning when I walked in in that cycling look. I felt like THAT BITCH and, if you want too much information, I was fully tucked for the first ever time with no underwear on. A MOMENT.

I remember security coming over and telling me that the model and muse Kyle Farmery and the legendary Amanda Lepore were inviting me to go sit with them. It felt like something out of *Mean Girls*. I had been invited to have drinks with the popular kids. I got escorted through the club by security and welcomed by Amanda's entourage before Amanda herself turned to me and told me I looked *sexy husky voice* gorgeous. Never one to show that I'm absolutely screaming inside, I partied with them and even had Amanda telling me that there's nothing more glam than seeing a bit of visible tape on show . . . Now I wish Amanda Lepore had been there on week one of *Drag Race*.

New York City in 2018 was the time in my life when I felt the most confident in who I was, my queer identity and my fashion. They all go hand in hand at allowing me to be who Bimini is today, and I have so many people to thank for that but especially Ella Lynch. Without her I'd probably still not be taking it seriously. We did it for ourselves and now we've done it on a global platform. Love that for us.

I love to chat with the universe. When I arrived in the red draped outfit Ella styled for our first ever look

together, I actually said: 'Next year I'll be walking the runway.' It happened.

When I put together the performance to 'Private Dancer' by Tina Turner I told myself I was going to win Miss Sink The Pink. It happened.

When I manifested that I was going to get into *Drag Race*, not only did it happen, but I also manifested that I would walk every single runway and make it to the final. It happened.

That was my biggest goal. To show every single outfit on that runway and prove to people that they should expect the unexpected.

I won't bore you by dissecting all of my runways. I've already told you all how you slept on the Norwich City look so we'll leave that as an honourable mention. I *am*, however, going to dissect my top three looks so you can see the reference points that are pulled for each look.

Bimini's Top Three Looks

In third place . . .

My final runway. The bridal punk. An Ella Lynch Creation. We wanted to go over the top for this finale extravaganza, but still bring in that slightly trashy element. I was running around every charity shop in East London searching for a wedding dress; I finally found a vintage eighties one for around £100. Ella took the appliqué off the dress and then customised a bespoke corset from Misty Couture (probably the best corset maker in the world), using parts of the original wedding dress and other components to make it extra, including a cheeky nipple in a little Westwood nod. The train was elegant. The hair choice was manufactured within an inch of its life, every hair flick and swoosh noted perfectly. The look pulled together references from Mugler to Rihanna and was topped off with my signature black smoky eye and glossy lip. Bridal for the finale might not make sense to all, but those fashion heads will understand the genius in it. I hope so.

In second place . . .

Prehistoric. My sexy cell. The bacteria that turns you queer. Created by Rickielee Drayford, an incredible designer and stylist in East London, whom I'm also lucky enough to call my friend. This came from me

thinking what prehistoric was and the easy route you could take. I traded bones and animal prints for the first life form. I took huge inspiration from the iconic designer Iris van Herpen. The way she creates silhouettes and designs that almost float as they move is mesmerising and I wanted to try to recreate that illusion. Rickie was up for the challenge, thankfully, and started sending ideas and designs that they thought feasible in the limited time we had. I paired it with another East London icon and designer Natacha Marro and her iconic nude bubble shoe. The shoe design is reminiscent of Alexander McQueen's Atlantis shoe, the wonderful shape it creates and the height it gives. I'm a sucker for a big shoe because I believe it can add such drama to an outfit. This was the week where I arrived as a real contender for the crown and earned my reputation with the judges and the audience as someone that will bring the unexpected. Paired with my Pricey win and runway victory, this look will always remain iconic to me. Like I said on the show ... if you don't get it right away, read a book.

Fun Fact: the hair for Prehistoric was originally going to be used for my finale outfit, but Ella wanted to change the finale hair during the lockdown filming hiatus and we realised how perfectly it fitted the brief for prehistoric. It was symmetrical and a bit weird and just *chef's kiss* worked.

Drum Roll PLEASE.

Stoned on the runway. The acne suit. A moment. This was one of those looks where my experimental style allowed Ella to push herself and it was a success. It was a bit gross but extremely editorial. Ella was inspired when using the stones on another suit and found they reminded her of spots and boils. There was an image of Bella Hadid knocking around wearing a sculpted Mugler outfit and Ella said to me – way before *Drag Race* – that she had an idea to put the stones on a flesh-toned 'Zit Suit'. So when I got the brief for *Drag Race*, I told Ella that we had to do it. Ella herself was reluctant at first; she was worried people wouldn't get it, but I wanted people to revel in the creativity of it. To this day I think of it as one of our best looks yet. I can't wait until I'm at some bitchy fashion party with my sunglasses on in my custom Ella Lynch Zit Suit. A crucial addition was the iconic Shirley Carter from *EastEnders*-style wig. That greasy, wet-look spiked mullet topped the look off and brought it to life. The wig was minging but that was the point. It was my standout look of the season and I'm so glad we went down that route. Again, the unexpected. Always.

As I've been writing this book, Ella and I have been plotting world domination. I've been doing a tonne of photoshoots and wearing some incredibly big designer labels but I realised quite quickly that I haven't got to where I am today by playing it the same as other people. Sure, some of these outfits are gorgeous and ridiculously

expensive . . . but anybody could wear them. To us, fashion is about going against the grain. I don't want to be a fashion darling, I want to be a fashion provocateur.

I'm grateful to have such creative people in my life that nourish my soul. We thrive for all of us to do better. Lifting each other up and creating work that will last is what it's about. Of course, this doesn't mean there aren't big name fashion icons in the mainstream who continue to influence and inspire me. To illustrate the point, here are some of my all-time favourites.

Bimini's Favourite Fashion Icons

Kate Moss

That's it. The ultimate icon. The supermodel with the cheeky London twang. My love for Kate goes deep. Deep enough to have a matching anchor tattoo on my right wrist. Recently I received a handwritten letter from Kate thanking me for my support and sending me a hoodie from her collection that raises money for the charity Sightsavers. I was ecstatic at the arrival of a letter rather than a restraining order.

Kate is self-aware. I have a sixth sense – it's like I have ESP or something. From years of having my finger on the beating pulse of pop culture I can tell that Kate knows what is going on. Now, anyway. Maybe a few years ago she was caught up in the hedonism of fame culture but she has been honest about it all. Partly because she had to be after having numerous scandals splashed across the front cover of national tabloids. Kate was always in on the joke, however, and never let the media's misogynistic tactics bring her down. A wild child whose weakness was having too much fun, she's strong enough to own her past mistakes (nothing tastes as good as owning up to your mistakes feels) but she's still successful after having her entire career ripped away. When Lee (his actual name) McQueen created the hologram of Kate Moss for his 2006 'Widows of Culloden' show in Paris it was instantly iconic. Lee was always working to go against the grain and do what was unexpected.

Kate is someone I look to today for inspiration. Her no-fucks-given attitude mixed with her cheek is something to behold. When she was signed as a model, she was three inches shorter than the legs-to-their-armpits supermodels we had seen before. She was young, fresh and unconventional when compared to the then-desirable attributes in fashion models. She had striking features, but she also had a boyish charm about her. She was quickly propelled into superstardom as her own entity, breaking the boundaries of what fashion was showing us and doing it a new kind of way.

Me and Kate are the same height. Go figure. We're kindred spirits. Actually, right now, we're like two ships in the night. There have been multiple instances when we were meant to have met but it hasn't happened . . . yet.

Most iconic moment: Opening up a new ideal of model for the nineties. Not conforming to what had been before her and creating her own path.

David Bowie

I'm ashamed to say that in my foolish adolescence I was more into the pop culture of my era and I disregarded both Bowie's music and his style. As I got into my mid-teens, say 15, I started to understand David Bowie for the nonconformist that he was. Bowie was a heartthrob, but not in your usual sex symbol type of way. There was something different about him. You can't deny his impact. He changed the face of music by being a rebel with a message and a heart. When it was still seen as sinful to be gay, Bowie told the world he was a homosexual, although his true sexuality has always been a mystery. Bowie was cunning with the media; even in more recent interviews before his tragic passing he would play the interviewers with his wit. Everything he did was for his music and his art. He dressed extravagantly and wore makeup. He was a provocateur, an icon. Long live his legacy. The man that fell from Mars and into our hearts.

Most iconic moment: He challenged how gender was represented throughout his career and built bridges for people to be themselves. Also the outfit he wore by Japanese fashion designer Kansai Yamamoto for his Aladdin Sane tour was pretty legendary.

Grace Jones

Hailing from Jamaica, Grace Jones is nothing short of an iconoclast. Grace is a rebellious pioneer who set the worlds of fashion, film and music on fire with aesthetics that broke categorisation and defied appropriation. What's

so mesmerising is how Grace's attachment to the zeitgeist is still so relevant today. She created this vision of who she is that was so true to herself. Grace has never fit into a binary. She wasn't overtly feminine or masculine, but also never felt the need to explain it. It's people like Grace and Bowie that have been smart enough to laugh back at the relentless questioning and label-pushing the mainstream always wants. Grace has never fit into a box and that nonconformity is hugely appealing. She moves with the times but transforms and transcends expectations.

Most iconic moment: Her general demeanour and spirit. She is hugely inspirational to me because there is something important to take from her today: not feeling like we have to explain ourselves to fit into certain categories that society expects of us. La Vie en Rose, forever.

Princess Julia

Princess Julia. A true legend, icon and trailblazer. I felt so bad about misrepresenting Julia on *Drag Race* as my UK Gay Icon but the reaction was everything I could have hope for. I remember having my nose stuck in a fashion book at the London College of Fashion when I studied there for a year in 2012. It's when I first discovered who Julia was after researching the vast history of British fashion and, like everyone, I was obsessed. They have witnessed every major fashion movement since the late seventies and have been an inspiration for many of those fashion trends. The blitz kids? Julia's impact. Julia wouldn't have remembered me when we first met because I was just another queer with a dream and a patchy hair colour but I remember being starstruck when I went to the George and Dragon (RIP) in East London and saw them behind the decks. Julia on the mic is as captivating as their style. I'm lucky enough to be friends with Julia now and we've interviewed each other for *i-D*. I've made it! As a pioneering legend of the East End and the true First Lady of Fashion I will never shut up about my adoration for Princess Julia.

Most iconic moment: Still being hailed as a fashion icon and STILL SERVING LOOKS. The kids could never.

Prince

Prince had an ecletic style. Unique, distinct and pretty sexy. In a rare interview he once said 'I wear what I want because I don't really like clothes.' Which is pretty iconic and I think I'm gonna steal that. He's another one, like Bowie, that fascinated me with their style and idea of being viewed as 'other'. Feminine and a bit of an alien. The mainstream saw Prince as this weird grey area when it came to style and fashion. He wore make-up and sung riddles about gender, sexuality and identity. He brought the conversation surrounding gender and fashion to more prominence all while wearing high heels and lace. He didn't give a fuck and neither should we!

Most iconic moment: Quite possibly the *Purple Rain* outfit. I think it's the first thing you think of when Prince is mentioned. The iconic outfit for an iconic tour.

Madonna

Would any queer inspiration be complete without the Queen of Pop herself? I grew up in a time that would shame Madonna for still being overtly sexy even though at the time she was in her mid forties. Madonna didn't give a fuck. It's Madonna. She can do what she wants and she knows it. As someone that is constantly inspired by reinvention, Madonna is the number one. She's played with loads of styles (some of which we wouldn't go near today, would we Madge?) and has always been 100 per cent unapologetic in her essence. To the core, Madonna is a true punk. She defies expectations of what is expected of her as a woman in pop culture. She's a provocateur. You only have to google Madonna's fashion to find countless articles of her 'most shocking outfits of all time'. A legend.

Most iconic moment: Never giving in to the patriarchy and doing it all her own way. Including a card in her *Like a Prayer* album called 'The Facts about AIDS'. 'People with AIDS – regardless of their sexual orientation – deserve compassion and support, not violence and bigotry.' Madonna showing herself to be a true ally . . .

Bimini's Favourite Fashion Designers

Vivienne Westwood

Environmental issues, human rights, climate change – Dame Vivienne Westwood is one of a kind. Her contribution to fashion should never be overlooked, sparking a revolution amongst the industry with her risqué, daring and unusual creations. The brand has some of my favourite fashion moments of all time, but that aside, the way Westwood uses her platform to be an advocate for climate change is pretty iconic. I'd recommend watching documentaries on her because she's an extremely fascinating women. She holds no bars in telling you exactly how she feels and has taken it upon herself to change the planet. Admittedly, having a big brand as successful as Westwood is flawed when it comes to genuinely getting your carbon footprint to a big, fat zero but at least she's trying. One of her famous quotes is 'Buy less, choose well and make it last!' She's now in her early eighties and still designs as much of her collection as possible but with a commitment to climate protection and human rights. She never considered herself a fashion designer but her use of tweeds, tartans, latex and corsetry allowed her to cement herself as a key fashion player. Everything Westwood designs must have a character, an opinion. When I'd read fashion magazines, I'd always be drawn to Westwood designs due to their unconventional nature.

She's donated millions to environmental charities. She uses her runways to make political statements 'Fracking is a crime', 'Austerity is a crime' and she calls on other labels to make the switch from fossil fuels to green energy. There are layers to Vivienne Westwood – her blunt and honest approach may sometimes be confusing but she hugely inspires me today.

Most iconic moment: Too many to choose but if I had to pick one . . . I'd say when she drove a military tank to David Cameron's home in a protest against fracking. I think I should take a leaf out of that book . . .

Alexander McQueen

May this icon be at peace and rest in the beauty of his creations. Always a provocateur and never one to do the obvious, McQueen's mind was its own heavenly genius. Isabella Blow knew McQueen was special and fought for his mainstream success before being sadly thrown out of the inner circle. McQueen's upbringing wasn't the easiest but he turned his experiences into walking art, often referencing childhood abuse and trauma in his work. No matter how famous he got, he never lost the rawness that people admired so highly. He didn't want people to see pretty clothes, he wanted people to feel them. His use of theatrics within his collections was part of the magic he was trying to evoke. His runways were exhilarating, weird, outrageous and often criticised for going too far. Perhaps he wasn't truly recognised until his tragic demise but his legacy will forever live on. It's that raw, unapologetic nature that truly inspires me.

Most iconic moment: Reviving Kate Moss' career by projecting the ghostly hologram of her in his 2006 'Widows of Culloden' show in Paris. It's when two worlds collide for me . . .

John Galliano

Another British designer that pushed boundaries, broke records and created some of the most breathtaking fashion moments in British history. Never one to do the ordinary, Galliano, at his peak, would take you on a journey of historical references and traditional silhouettes with an edge. Obviously it helps that he is so fabulously queer and I also did a campaign for Margiela, which is headed up by Galliano. He's been controversial, cancelled and called-out for some quite revolting exclamations which he blamed on his addiction to drink and drugs. Thankfully he's been on the road to recovery and has been extremely apologetic about his past behaviour. Controversy aside, his vision is unparalleled.

Most iconic moment: Princess Diana wearing Galliano's first creation for Dior. The lingerie-inflected, sapphire gown worn by Diana as she went to the Dior exhibition at the MET. I mean Galliano has done so much but I do love me some Di.

FASHION

IS ABOUT GOING

AGAINST THE

MOULD

Life Lesson 6:
Love Yourself, Say that Again

Terms like 'self-love' and 'self-care' have grown in popularity over the last couple of years. Everyone's seen one of those pastel pink Instagram posts about loving yourself, or passed someone on the Tube carrying a tote bag with a quote about self-care. But the origins of these concepts are much deeper than just having a bubble bath, lighting a scented candle or taking some time out of your schedule for masturbation.

The idea of self-love, particularly for queer people, is hundreds of years old and focuses on learning to take better care of ourselves in a hostile world – one where we are expected to fight constantly for our right to exist. Shakespeare hinted at the idea in *Othello* when the character Iago says, 'Our bodies are our gardens, to which our wills are gardeners', followed by Oscar Wilde in the 1890s who wrote, 'To love oneself is the beginning of a lifelong romance.' The modern idea of self-care for activists, though, can mostly be traced back to Black feminists such as Audre Lorde who wrote 'Caring for myself is not self-indulgence . . . It is self-preservation, and that is an act of political warfare.' What she was talking about as a Black lesbian feminist was the need to care for yourself in a world that is constantly hostile towards you.

AUDRE LORDE

In this chapter, I want to share how I've learned to take better care of myself over the years. To do that, I want to dive into some of the darker experiences I've had, in particular with mental health and addiction issues. For some people, this might be a bit close to home or heavy and so if it's not for you feel free to skip this section!

I don't have all the answers about self-love, but in order to share some of my experiences I want to take you back to my childhood years again, and talk about how young Bimini was a bit of a natural hedonist. I remember being eight or nine and hearing trance music like '9pm (Till I Come)' by ATB and 'Insomnia' by Faithless on the radio and thinking, 'I can't wait to go to Ibiza and take loads of

drugs and party and live that life'. When I visited the Talk to Frank website about drugs aged 12 or 13, I'd be reading the health advice, but only ever looking at the interesting effects of every substance. Clearly, I was up for fun but perhaps not as concerned about balance, or the price paid for excess. Later in my teens I started smoking weed and taking the odd pill recreationally. But it was only when I got to university that I really jumped off the wagon.

In previous chapters, I mentioned how in my first year of university I was partying every night. Inevitably, this meant being around drugs. On the London queer scene at the time – 2014 and 2015 – as well as the usual clubbing drugs like cocaine and ecstasy, two other substances were popular. One was mephedrone, a stimulant previously sold online, a 'legal high' that the government criminalised back in 2010. The other was a drug referred to on the scene as G (short for GHB), a liquid depressant that can produce feelings of disinhibition and euphoria but which also carries with it a relatively high risk of overdose, unconsciousness, coma and death.

If you don't do drugs, you might wonder why anyone would take something with those risks, but it was very normalised within the scene I was a part of. At first, I was just as wary as you'd imagine: I remember being at parties with my friends and seeing people do G. Sometimes people would pass out and I thought 'I'll never take that; it's not good news.' Yet, somewhat inevitably, I eventually started taking it. Unfortunately, like many things that can be bad for you, I loved it. I would party for days and keep taking it to keep riding the feelings of euphoria. The lack of sleep soon started to really fuck me up (to use a clinical term). A friend once told me that after several days on drugs they would start to hear voices and I cockily thought 'that never happens to me'. Then it did. That's where things started to get dark. I wasn't as strong as I thought I was.

GHB is a dangerous drug and it took hold of me. You aren't meant to drink alcohol with it so I spent the majority of this time alcohol-free. There was a big percentage of queer people that got lost in G's grasp. I never really used it as a sexual drug though. It's often associated with chemsex which wasn't really my scene. Quite often we'd see people fucking at the parties we were at but everyone was so high they didn't really care. I'd be jumping around wearing next to nothing playing pop music, or something a bit heavier. I remember one of my darkest moments after a bender when I finally slept; every hour my body would wake up, shaking. I get a bit emotional thinking about it because I was so lost. The reason I was waking up every hour is because that's when you would take a shot of G, hourly. At that moment, I saw the light and knew I needed help.

Addiction looks different in everyone. Sometimes we assume addicts are people who can never manage their own lives and things fall apart for them. The thing is, though, some addicts can continue to function in most of their daily life, which allows them to avoid confronting the harm an addiction is doing. I always had the idea that if I was only taking drugs in a party atmosphere, I was fine. That logic doesn't work when you're partying for 80 per cent of your week. It was fun at the start but my entire second year of university was a blur. I just about passed my course, but I got really sick. I wasn't eating. I developed ulcers in my colon (glamorous, I know). I knew deep down that I was so unwell because of the drugs, but with the doctors I pretended I had no idea what the cause was. As soon as I stopped taking drugs, of course, all the physical ailments cleared up pretty quickly. I also went vegan, so there's that too.

I remember having an out-of-body experience once. It was not long after the G alarm clock episode happened and this is when I began to realise that I couldn't do it anymore. It was in that drifting stage of sleep, and I still don't know whether it was sleep paralysis or not, but a voice spoke to me. The reason I don't think it was sleep paralysis is because this voice was serene. It was comforting. It was warm. I've had sleep paralysis in the past and it's been terrifying – a cackling banshee attacking me in my own home. This was the opposite of that.

I can't really remember whether I saw anything visual but I felt this powerful energy. It washed over me. The voice told me the path I was on was not the right path and I had angels trying to guide me away from where I was. The voice had other things to say but for the sake of not sounding like an absolute nutjob I'll keep those things to myself. It told me what I already knew – I couldn't live this way anymore.

I often think back to that moment and question whether I'd accidentally ingested lots of ketamine. It was weird, but it was affirming. Maybe I've got angels looking out for me or maybe I was just tripping balls; either way, it triggered a flight response in my psyche and I knew that was it.

When I decided to do something about my addiction, I knew I needed a reset. My lifestyle in London wasn't sustainable: for me it was always 'all or nothing' – I was a party monster. So I'd need another reinvention, and that meant leaving London to go travelling for six months between my second and final years of university. It's one of the times in my life where I truly believe the universe was on my side, because my landlord in London brought the tenancy to an end early, leaving me with the financial ability to get out for a bit. I went back to my mum's and regained a sense of normality. Then I used some of my student loan to go to South East Asia. It was the best decision I ever made. If I had continued using drugs the way I was, I'm pretty sure I wouldn't be alive right now – it had reached that point. I consider myself lucky because I was ultimately able to stop completely, but the effects of my time using drugs had changed my social skills. Once I stopped, if I was in a social situation and not high, I was so uncomfortable. I had lost the ability to be social without drink or drugs – I forgot what you were supposed to do in these situations. I was convinced that no one liked me and no one thought I was fun. Social anxiety, basically. It wasn't fun: I really got in my own head and was quite paranoid. It's taken a few years of working on myself to get that back and now I am able to go into a room and have fun without drink and drugs, but the transition period wasn't easy.

While I want to be open about my experiences, it's important to talk about shame and stigma, which affect queer and trans people because of our identities but also affect people with addiction issues too. My own history of drug addiction aside, I don't think this country's attitude to drugs is the right one. Criminalising drugs has clearly failed as a strategy and only increases stigma. People will use drugs recreationally anyway – often without becoming addicts – and treating it as a crime instead of a health issue doesn't help anyone. We should be funding better support services, outreach and counselling in the community instead. While drug use is higher in some LGBTQ+ communities compared to straight communities, I think it's important not to paint queer people as especially hedonistic or 'troubled'. It's important to have a healthy discussion in the community about these issues but without shaming people. Also, straight people take drugs too! Plenty of cishet city suits are banging cocaine every weekend and no one frames the drugs discussion as being a problem for the straight community. The only difference I think is that queer people are often trying to find connection and community in a world not designed for us to thrive in. Straight people might be doing drugs at the weekend but then they go back to their mortgages and families and it's all good. Some people in the queer and trans community face more difficulties and discrimination, which means it can be easier to get caught up in escapism. My philosophy is that whether someone drinks or uses drugs or not, we all need a personal level of balance – like two scales. I lost that when I was younger and have worked to get it back up. Imagine if I was a Gemini!

The reality is that most of us already know on a rational level what we should be doing to take care of ourselves: we should be exercising, drinking two litres of water a day, eating healthily and socialising. The problem is it can be hard on a practical and emotional level to do it all. Often it will be unattainable, but we need to be kind to ourselves and try to do the best we can. We're in a weird climate right now, with a pandemic still looming and life as we once knew it completely dishevelled. There's an increasing urge to be super-productive, often spurred on by watching others on social media and thinking we need to be doing more. Frankly, we're all exhausted. This toxic productivity trend doesn't serve anyone other than capitalism. This idea that we should 'work hard, play hard' creates unrealistic goals for our own wellbeing. Let me tell you first hand, I'm struggling. I've been thrust into this new world and I'm trying to navigate with a lot more eyes on me than before, but I'm still the same person I was nine months ago. I'm grateful as fuck for the life I'm living now, but I can find it hard to disconnect sometimes. With our lifestyles and our phones, we're always connected. Our circadian rhythms are all skew-whiff. I've fallen victim to toxic productivity and I need to follow my own advice.

These won't work for everyone but here are some of the small ways I try and show myself love and care in order to maintain my own balance:

1. Setting goals

Some days the goals you might set may be serving girl-boss realness with checklists, meetings and deadlines you rush to meet. On others it might be as basic as getting out of bed and brushing your teeth. Our self-care goals don't always have to be significant if we're feeling down: just clear and achievable.

2. Exercise

I want to inspire you to try a new form of exercise. Be confident and throw yourself into it (you can find queer-focused ones if that makes you more comfortable). Looking after the body is important in looking after the mind. It isn't always easy. I get angry at myself when I compromise exercise. It's about finding that balance that works for you. Put on your headphones and go for a run. Get sexy and sweat but don't do it for anyone other than yourself.

3. Meditation

I struggled with this at first but when it's on, it's on. I find I can centre myself much more after a workout but they don't have to be mutually exclusive. It isn't always easy to find the time to sit still and focus on your thoughts. There are great apps like Headspace that can offer courses for you to follow. I find guided meditations to be the most effective in keeping my focus strong. Meditation helps to calm you. It's a great practice to try do as regularly as possible.

4. Music

Madonna. That's it. She's got an entire catalogue that is probably a hundred hours long. That's a hundred hours of pure pop bliss. If you don't like Madonna, I don't know what else to say. Putting a new album, an old album, your favourite playlist or radio station on can help to lift your spirit. There's nothing like shaking your ass to Fatboy Slim to make your worries go away!

5. Clearing my physical environment

The previous tip goes side by side with this. Put the music on and clear it up honey. I'm sometimes pretty rubbish at this, but when I have everything in order I feel a lot lighter. It can be overwhelming to work as an artist where a lot of things I use end up on the floor. Ella is always telling me off for being messy but I know when everything is tidy it helps to calm me down. Light a candle as well! Lavender is my favourite.

6. Masturbation

We all do it. We all have different fantasies or ways of making ourselves cum. I'd invest in toys if you want to try something new. Experiment. Use your imagination as well. Porn can be fine but it has unrealistic sexual boundaries and can have a knock-on effect on your own sex life. If you're wanting to get horny, use your brain. I like to have an orgasm every single day if I can.

7. Having healthy boundaries

You can take from this what resonates with you. Whether it's food, sex or substances: it's about finding a balance and knowing when you need to rein it in. Trust me, this is coming from a person that went so far one way they didn't know they were going to come back. Do everything you want, but in moderation and not excess.

8. Checking in on your loved ones

This might seem obvious but when was the last time you had a conversation with your family? We can get so caught up in our lives – being busy, overworking, undereating – that we forget to catch up with the people we love. Family, friends, chosen family – whoever makes you happy, call them. It might be the antidote you need.

9. Getting a yoga practice

There is a form of yoga for everybody, and the wonders it can do for your mind and body are incomparable. Whether you're a complete beginner or you've got some experience, trying to stick to a regular practice helps to maintain a balance in your soul. I was an avid yogi, every single morning, and now that's been compromised by my work schedule. But doing it once or twice a week is better than not doing it at all. Always remember that with everything, showing up is the hardest part.

10. Being kind to yourself

Could this be the most important motto to live by? We're not perfect; perfection doesn't exist. Don't try to strive to be anything other than your authentic self. We all want to be the best version we can but that involves taking time out and stripping back to basics. Turn your phone off, take a deep breath and dance around. You're much better when you feel less stressed.

Bimini's Guide to Coming Out

For some people in the LGBTQ+ community, an important part of their queer journey to self-love is coming out to some or all of the people in their life. Coming out is a complex, lifelong process and it isn't always a part of everyone's journey. Some people can't come out for reasons of safety, while others just don't feel the need to – and that's perfectly okay. Do what works for you, and you only. Coming out, for me, was an important part of the process of fully embracing my queerness and loving myself. No one ever really prepared me for it, told me how to do it, or how many times I'd have to do it, and to be honest it's bloody nerve-racking (and still is). So for those reading who might be thinking about diving out of the closet and releasing the beast, here's my two cents.

'Coming out' can be scary. It's a stupid process that the patriarchy (again!) has made necessary by insisting that everyone should be assumed to be boring unless they specify otherwise. Remember when famous pop stars like Stephen Gately or Will Young, or actors like Ellen DeGeneres did front-page cover stories with headlines like 'MY TRUTH' as they explained to the public that they had embraced the lifestyle choice of homosexuality. I actually think it gave the normies the idea that you come out once and that's it. The truth is queer and trans people have to come out constantly – every time you mention your partner at the office water cooler or tell

the *Vogue* photographer 'it's they/them, actually'. The thing is, though, we shouldn't even need to come out. Having to come out reinforces the idea that everyone is straight by default. Lots of people can't be out for various reasons and I don't think it's helpful to suggest their experience is fake or that they're being deceptive. In a healthier society, we might not make assumptions about someone's sexuality at all, or everyone might be queer or non-binary and your identity would be about as much of a discussion point as your eye colour.

I came out once. I came out again. Then I came out once more after that. I came out yesterday to the Uber driver. We're constantly coming out as something. Growing up, it was naturally assumed that I was straight. That's always the default, right? Straight until proven otherwise. Then I opted for bisexual because I think I felt it to be right for me at the time. Then I moved to London and was fully homosexual until I started experimenting with my gender identity and then I came out as non-binary. The homosexual and non-binary parts were probably the easiest because of the company I kept. Nobody batted a false eyelash. Then I came out as non-binary to the entire world on national television. That was quite something.

I'm going to come out to you all again now. I realise that my sexuality is fluid. I'm pansexual, which is the physical attraction to kitchenware. My particular kink is copperware. I just love a brassy finish.

I jest. Pansexual means that your sexual attractions are not limited by a person's biological sex, gender expression or gender identity. Basically, it's the attraction to people of all genders. It's the even 'greedier' version of being bisexual, which is something I often got called. 'You're just greedy, pick one.' No, Sharon, I don't want to pick one. Would you buy one lipstick if there were plenty of lipsticks on offer?

I'm a lot more sexually assured now. I think. I found that the biggest obstacle when trying to dive out of the closet was my own thoughts. The sense of relief you feel once you've admitted to another human how you're feeling inside is huge. Coming out requires the use of language which is forever evolving. Even though a lot of these different ideas about sexuality and gender identity have

existed forever, we now have more nuanced terminology with which to openly discuss them. The dialogue has changed.

I do want to share some tips and advice for coming out, though, because it's an important part of the wider theme of self-love as a queer person. And I'm somewhat of an expert, as someone who has had to do it a few times . . .

1. No matter how you come out, it'll be embarrassing

Not at the time, necessarily, but talking about your identity is such an earnest, sincere thing to do that it inevitably means you'll look back a few years later when you don't care anymore and fucking cringe. The memory of the florid letter you wrote your parents, or the crying hug you had with your bestie will start to make you wince. Why couldn't you have been more chill? The thing is, that's totally normal. Coming out is an awkward process we shouldn't even need to go through anyway and so no matter how any of us do it it's never going to be fully right. An analogy I'd use is tattoos – when you get a tattoo you spend ages agonising over the right choice; the reality is you almost certainly will end up embarrassed by whatever it is. But bad tattoos are part of your story and learning to live with them is part of growing up. So be kind to yourself about the choices you make. Perhaps try to avoid screaming it across the Christmas dinner table though. It's a bit *EastEnders*.

2. Talk to someone you trust

While it might seem efficient to make up a bunch of fly-ers which say, 'Janice Ian: dyke' or similar and then distribute them around the school corridors à la Regina George, I think this probably isn't wise for your own mental health. The first few reactions you get for being a queer will stick with you for life and it's best to start only with people you already trust. Family can be a com-plicated one – especially if your family have not been every welcoming of queerness in their own lives or are maybe religious. For some people, Mum and Dad will be the first people they tell and for others their parents will simply never know, yet all their mates will. Whether it's a friend or relative, try to share your feelings first with someone you know won't judge you, won't expect you to have all of the answers and who absolutely will not tell anyone you don't want them to tell. That last point is really important: we all had someone at school who got outed to the whole year by someone they trusted. It's not good, so pick carefully.

3. You don't have to be out in all areas of your life

'Coming out' isn't a one-off process. Think about most celebrities who identify as LGBTQ+. When they come out publicly in the press it's usually been a well-known industry 'secret' for years. They might have a 'personal trainer' who is regularly in paparazzi shots with them, or be using neutral pronouns with their management and we are none the wiser. It's the same for everyone. Some people choose to be out at work but not at home and for others it's the reverse. That's fine, it's YOUR choice and about where you feel safe and comfy sharing yourself. No one is owed an explanation of your truth and you deserve to find your people and share only what you're comfortable with.

4. You can change your mind

I am queer, gender nonconforming and non-binary but I suppose when I first came out a lot of people would have thought I was a gay man – and I probably went along with that. Lots of people come out as one thing, have a rethink later down the line and come out again as something else. It's completely common and not something you've got 'wrong': identity is complex and fluid and language and ideas about gender and sexuality are ever-evolving. It's actually a positive if you are constantly reinterpreting yourself in light of new information. Don't let others impose labels on you or shame you for being 'confused'. It IS confusing sometimes but it can also be fun to be inconsistent and contradict yourself.

Wouldn't it be boring if we all just picked one label and kept it forever?

5. If you get a negative reaction . . .

The truth is, coming out wouldn't be so hard if everyone was cool with queers. For some people, coming out will get a negative reaction, which can be painful especially if from family and friends. Be kind to yourself but also remember that people sometimes say and do things when they're in shock or when they don't fully understand something. Sometimes, people need time to reflect, do some thinking, educate themselves or just calm the fuck down before they can be their best for the LGBTQ+ people in their lives. Don't be a doormat if someone is being an asshole but try to practise forgiveness if someone who means a lot to you apologises and tries to make amends for a shitty first reaction. Life is short so why not give someone the option to admit they fucked up and try to be an ally.

6. NEVER 'out' someone

This applies even if you're LGBTQ+ yourself, or they're your best friend, or your dog. It is never okay to out someone without their permission and you should always check with other people about how they want their identity discussed publicly – especially if they come out to you. Outing people is easily done and sometimes more thoughtless than mean-spirited, but it has the potential to harm someone. Badly. We all should try to be kinder to each other and exercise respect for anyone else who is marginalised, oppressed or struggling because of the patriarchy, their sexuality and gender roles.

7. There are no right or wrong ways to come out

Don't ever feel like you have to follow a rulebook or method, because there isn't one. There are over 7 billion people on the planet. Like I said, I've come out numerous times. I struggled to navigate it. It's important to find the strength within yourself before you dive out of the wardrobe and into the uncharted terrain of Narnia. Whether you write a letter, tell people face to face, or come out publicly on social media so that it's all done and everyone knows at once . . . just find the way that works for you.

8. Time is a social construct; tear it apart

Okay, maybe time isn't *entirely* a social construct like gender. We know about the sun and the moon but if you don't know about the birds and the bees yet, that's okay. Whether you're 14, or 44, or 84 . . . there is no time pressure or limit on coming out. When I spoke publicly about being non-binary, I received messages from people in their sixties telling me that what I said resonated with them for the first time ever. They felt like they could truly be themselves after hearing a rhetoric that fit them. Don't feel pressured by seeing other people coming out; follow your heart and only do it at a time that's right for you.

*

I hope we can get to a point where the assumed sexuality for everyone isn't straight. Straight people don't have to come out because the world is on their side already. I admit that I don't know everything about gender and sexuality – no one does. It's all down to individual choice and preference and that's how it should be taught. I often think about how queer people don't get to be fully themselves until they are a lot older. How much amazing talent are we missing out on because queer people didn't get their passions nourished due to the pressures of conformity and heteronormative expectations?

The younger generation are becoming a lot more open and attuned to all of the different ways that people identify. It's great. It's mostly the Karens of the world who have a problem but that's only a reflection of that generation. Children are impressionable and learn behaviours. Homophobia, queerphobia, transphobia, racism and sexism are all learned behaviours; kids are generally not racist or transphobic until they're taught to be.

I have a transgender sibling and a lesbian sibling, both under the age of 15. The fact that they both have the courage to come out only reinforces the change happening in society and it excites me. We're moving into a territory where the battle around language is causing division within our own community. Parts of the LGBTQ+ community are getting annoyed at the acronym becoming longer, but the plus has always stood for all of the other underrepresented parts of the community. LGBT has never meant *just* LGBT.

I'm queer as folk, mate, and I couldn't be prouder.

Life Lesson 7:
Watch What You Put in Your Mouth

How'd you know someone's vegan?
They'll tell you.

I've been vegan since 2015. That's six years without consuming cheese or snacking on a chicken wing. Well, at least dairy cheese or flesh chicken anyway. I went vegan for a number of reasons which I'll discuss a bit further on . . . but mainly for my health and for ethical reasons. Thank fuck vegan food has stepped its cookies up because when I first took the plunge, the cheese tasted like cardboard and everything had milk powder in. WHY DID EVERYTHING HAVE MILK POWDER IN? The dairy industry must have had some weird satanic deal with every brand that meant they had to include 0.3 per cent of this unnecessary shit in everything they made. In this chapter, I'm going to be as unpreachy as possible, though I can't say I won't be sarcastic as hell, and I'm happy for you to take everything I say in this one with a pinch of salt. I'm not standing at a Tube station shouting hateful rhetoric into a megaphone. I'm sitting at home drinking a coffee with a splash of oat milk (I swapped titty milk for a plant alternative way before I went fully vegan).

My dad is also a vegan. A vocal one. I remember going

on to his Facebook and seeing that he had shared a post referring to himself as a Hummusexual. The epitome of a vegan dad joke. I also witnessed him heckling a lot of people who disagreed with his choice (and vice versa) to ditch dairy and meat and live plant-based. My dad is intelligent with a sarcastic wit; he knows exactly how to wind people up. It was entertaining to watch angry, gammon-faced blokes get riled up about veganism and use stereotypical anti-vegan comebacks like BACON, THOUGH and WHY DO WE HAVE CANINES THEN? These are typical knee-jerk reactions, often used in retaliation when confronted by someone like my dad talking about the cruelty of animal farming, or the fact that you'd likely never human drink breast milk after you stop counting your age in months so why do we drink the milk that is biologically compatible with a baby cow?

What's interesting about the canine analogy is when you consider the size of our canine teeth compared to those of wild carnivorous animals. If I took a bite out of my arm the likelihood is I would recoil from the pain but I doubt I'd be able to tear through the flesh as easily as a lion would. Funnily enough, the largest canine teeth on any living animal belong to a herbivore (the hippopotamus, in case you're wondering), so sorry Steve mate, but that argument's null and void.

One thing about my dad's Facebook social activism was how gruelling it must have been. I know it helped some people make the switch but it also helped decrease my dad's Facebook friends list. Constantly going back and forth with people who don't agree with you over a subject you feel passionate about is exhausting. It's the dark side of social media where people can spout their views and argue with people they disagree with. I would say my dad was quite the antagonist and he probably got off on pissing people off. Rather like me pissing people off by getting my arse out in a tartan skirt.

I'd never say my dad was preachy but he definitely fell victim to the vegan stereotype. People think we spurt nothing more than propaganda and have a self-righteous perspective on everyone else. While the latter is probably true for a lot of vegans, I never wanted to be like that. How can we expect people to make a connection with veganism when we've been brought up in a culture that gives us access to meat at every meal? My mum would tell me that when she grew up, they'd have meat just two or three times a week. It would usually be a roast and then leftovers would be made into something else, or turned into a soup. Meat just wasn't as cheap and accessible as it is now.

Social conditioning isn't just limited to gender. It extends to various other learned behaviours in society, including the food we consume. Why would we ever question where our food came from or whether we should be drinking a certain type of milk if it's all we've ever known? After my parents divorced, my dad got bitten by the vegan vamp when he was well into his fifties, while my mum's side of the family are liberal-traditional Scots who dine on meat and two veg. I grew up with my dad competing for the title of World's Fastest Eater at every meal we had. He'd devour his steak, rare. An ex-bodybuilder, in the eighties he'd drink gallons of milk and eat dozens of eggs each day to get his protein fix. Meat and dairy were a big part of my working-class upbringing, so when I wanted to turn vegetarian around the age of nine it was disregarded and quickly brushed under the carpet by my mum. I remember being told I was being fed vegetarian Quorn for at least a year before realising I'd been lied to the entire time.

Some vegans can't stand the taste of meat. I'm not one of those vegans; I loved nothing more than greasy fried chicken and a pizza covered in melted cheese. It was a sacrifice I had to make because the feelings of guilt I had overpowered anything else.

I also used to have disgustingly inconvenient bowel problems. I told you it was for ethical AND health reasons. Politicians talk shit every day so I'm not afraid to talk about my colon.

'You can be vegetarian when you no longer live in this house!'

'You can be a bloody veggie when you cook your own meals!'

So that's exactly what I did. I'm not trying to say I was perfect but I always loved animals and made the connection between eating them and loving them as a contradiction quite young. I would cuddle my dog Ellie, our gorgeous family pet (a Shar Pei who lived a long life, considering they usually don't due to problems with pedigree breeding) and say, 'I could never eat you, so why would I eat a cow?'

I think it was difficult for my mum when I stopped eating meat and even more difficult when I fully gave up dairy. She felt betrayed, almost. I remember her saying, 'Was the food I gave you growing up not good enough?', which I can't understand fully as I am not a mother of a child but I can see how that would have made her feel. My mum went without so that me and my siblings could have the best of everything; we always had a cooked dinner on the table every single night, something I'm truly grateful for. I know how lucky I am and I never wanted to feel ungrateful or make her feel bad about it.

It was just a switch I had to do, consciously, to make myself feel better.

Whenever I would openly discuss with my mum the reasons why I didn't want to eat animals, she got it. Social conditioning aside, my mum is very nurturing and loving. When Disco's (my dog) mother Bella had puppies, my mum worked so hard day and night to ensure all the puppies got everything they needed. Bella didn't have to do anything basically. When I talk about animal cruelty, she would recoil and say she didn't want to hear it. At our core, we're empathetic beings that hate inequality, discrimination and any form of abuse to another sentient being. That's why we don't WANT to watch animals being tortured at a factory farm. We'd rather turn a blind eye than take on the guilt of witnessing what bacon goes through before it ends up in your butty. What I always think when I watch those exposés is how much stress must be going through that animal's body right now . . . the levels of fear they experience before death surely can't be good hormones to be putting into our body? Maybe that's why the middle-aged white blokes we sometimes call gammons are all red in the face . . .

We have such a disassociation with animal products that when we walk down the meat aisle in a supermarket, we don't acknowledge the suffering that has happened before the flesh is wrapped in the plastic film. Another argument you hear is how it's natural for us to eat meat because we're at the top of the food chain, so we're entitled . . . although I'd rather slice a carrot than be locked in a cage with a hungry tiger. We're intelligent, admittedly, and able to create weapons and machines that make us far more advanced than the rest of the animal kingdom, but when it comes down to natural selection you aren't going to get a plastic-wrapped chicken breast pumped with steroids in the jungle.

Let's put it this way: if you were locked in a room with a sheep, some vegetables and a stove would you be able to kill the sheep with your bare hands?

Let's talk about my gut! It's healthy to have a conversation about this part of our bodies, even though it's viewed as embarrassing. We often hide those parts of our life because we're afraid of judgement and because society has told us that oversharing isn't sexy. This very fear prevented me from seeing a doctor after years of self-diagnosed 'IBS' that later turned out to be something much worse.

In my late teens my body was going through a lot of changes, not helped by my occasional recreational drug use and unhealthy lifestyle choices. One thing I noticed was that I had a recurring pain in my stomach, almost daily, which resulted in me having to use the little enby's room

more frequently than one would have liked. As a queer person exploring their sexuality, this was a problem.

My friends and I would laugh at it. I was quite lucky that my best friend also suffered from a version of IBS so we comforted each other. It was – as I then thought – a condition that I would have to live with and so I did the proper British thing . . . pulled up my socks and got on with it.

When I was about 21 I remember I had been on a big bender and I went back to Norfolk. I was in excruciating pain; I had never felt pain like it. I still remember it now – sharp knife-like stabbing in my abdomen that would make me keel over in anguish. I'd had similar pains but never this severe. They were always . . . manageable, to an extent. This time it was torture. I finally did what I should have done years before and booked to see a gastroenterologist.

Fast-forward to the results of my colonoscopy (I remember enjoying the medication and reading the notes that said 'inserted without discomfort'). They told me that I was moderately lactose-intolerant and that dairy was covering my colon in ulcers. Mmm, sexy! I was diagnosed with ulcerative colitis, told that I would have the occasional 'flare-ups' and that it could develop into a worse condition, so to keep an eye on it.

'But you don't have to stop having dairy.'

That didn't add up to me. If I'm moderately intolerant to lactose and dairy has been cited as a trigger . . . why should I continue to eat it? It was a case of that tricky 'trust your doctor but also listen to your common sense' dilemma.

It didn't seem like it made much sense so I vowed to cut dairy out of my diet completely.

At this point I was already vegetarian so cutting out dairy was an easy transition, right? WRONG. I was fully on the cheese flex. Cheese was my biggest weakness, over any meat dish. It was just so bloody good in pasta and pizza and just everything . . . but within 20 minutes of deep-throating a calzone I'd be straight on the toilet quicker than Boris Johnson says 'I do!'

It took around six months to fully pander to my plant-based needs. The process seems slow but now it's second nature and it doesn't cross my mind.

And get this: since I stopped eating dairy, I've never had another flare-up. My bowel movements are regular and I'm

not in daily excruciating pain after having a bowl of Cheerios. Oat milk is my god and the cows live happily ever after.

Moral of the story – follow your gut. Do things for you and remember: even if you don't get there right away, if you keep aiming for the stars you'll get there eventually. Or at least turn vegan.

Ahh. The hypocrisy of being into fashion and then also promoting environmental practices. The two notoriously don't go hand in hand, unfortunately. I will say though, younger designers that are coming up through the fashion ranks are a lot more eco-conscious than before. Where it used to be seen as gimmicky, a joke, or that you'd stink like Nag Champa and tobacco, climate change and environmental awareness is now in fashion.

That's why fast fashion brands are trying to launch sustainable products out of recycled goods. They know the shit they're doing to the planet isn't forgiving, not to mention the human rights issues that come with buying a T-shirt in a sale for less than a pound. We're aware of this, but much like animal cruelty, because it isn't directly affecting us, we get on with our lives, pay our taxes and

occasionally go out and get slaughtered in a lovely new outfit that will likely not last you to the end of the evening.

It isn't our fault and I'm not blaming us. I'm blaming THEM. The higher powers that knew that the plastic they were creating wasn't going to go anywhere. The ones that compete with each other to sell the cheapest garment at the cost of the planet.

Now I'm not a saint. I've definitely bought pieces from fast fashion houses before. Even shopping on the high street has its issues. Humans aren't sustainable, no matter how much we throw the word in front of it. Sustainability has become a buzzword for many corporations – a bit like Pride and LGBTQ+ awareness – these companies don't give a shit but as long as they stick the word in front of anything they do to make it look like they're aware, it's okay.

I really try my hardest to be as conscious as I can. I'd love to ban single-use plastic globally but I haven't harnessed that power yet. When I order something for a look and it comes in plastic wrapping, it pisses me off. When I get sent a PR package that is filled with crap, or is a stupid size, it pisses me off. But I'm a consumer, so I'm part of the problem, and I can't act like I'm not. We all contribute to it but it's about actively trying to be aware of where it's coming from.

Basically, oil was the worst discovery ever and humans are a parasite on the planet, leeching off it until Mother Nature decides to freeze us over or try kill us off with a deadly virus.

I think if I keep in Mother's good books, hopefully she'll spare me.

She'll say, 'Bim, you haven't eaten a factory-farmed animal in many, many years so you have lowered your carbon footprint and helped minimise greenhouse emissions that were making it really hard for me to breathe, resulting in me warming up until I couldn't take it anymore. Sure, you have a lot of clothes but at least they're going to be archived in a museum for people to look at for years to come (manifesting here) so, tell you what, how about you make yourself a lovely cup of green tea and wait this one out.'

That's why I try not to wear leather. Although I've known that leather production is bad for the environment, so is making synthetic leather. It's all a minefield that the above average citizen can't navigate. As leather is usually a by-product of food waste, people don't think of it as an issue. But did you know that up to 50 per cent of natural leather hide is wasted and often destined for landfill? That's a shit-tonne of leather being wasted each year.

I think to be truly sustainable at this point we're at now, we should stop leather production completely and upcycle everything we've already created. It scares me the amount of waste we dispose of each year. Without sounding like the hippy dippy child I once was, like don't have a cow . . . ever!

Without trying to sound like a total patronising git, we've fucked it but it isn't entirely our fault. It's . . . DING you guessed it, CAPITALISM and THE PATRIARCHY!

Now let's dismantle it and sort this mess out before hell gets frozen over.

Life Lesson 8:
Get Bent

Although I was naturally athletic growing up, I was shit at all the things I was meant to be good at and good at all the things I was meant to be bad at. Going back through those awkward moments in high school and right up to more recent awkward moments in gyms, in this chapter I'm going to discuss the difficulties of navigating the very gendered world of fitness when you don't fit in, and why the hell the majority of us queers avoid it like a polka-dot dress.

We're all aware of the benefits fitness and exercise have on the soul. I know it sounds wanky but unfortunately it is true. If only we could look like a lingerie model and still deepthroat a burger and chips or swig a bottle of Pinot every night. Actually fuck it, we can look like a lingerie model by doing all those things. I retract that. Normalise representing all types of bodies in lingerie campaigns please, Ann Summers!

I don't engage in fitness because I want a banging body (although having a cracking arse isn't a terrible side effect), I do it because it helps quieten the little voice in my head. That's another side effect. Endorphins. As an ex-party monster, I'm always searching for a light buzz on a Tuesday afternoon. I know first-hand that entering that world of dumbbells and dumb boys can be off-putting, but the positive effects outweigh the negatives. Fitness is the best addiction I've ever had. Even as I write this that addiction has dwindled because my diary means I'm a (d)rag doll, but I still exercise as much as physically possible. Downward doggy counts, right?

Back when I was a kid, I broke two of my middle fingers playing football. Isn't that the most homosexual thing you've ever heard? In that transitional period between middle and high school, when we're 'experimenting', I tried my literal hand at football and ended up making the entire match about me, naturally. The lads jeered as the school teachers rushed around my fallen, shivering body as I lay on the floor, purple from the bleak winter weather. Turns out I was pretty shit at football, despite trying my hardest to be good. I'm secretly a competitive person by nature so this was a hard pill to swallow. I had to admit it – football didn't come as naturally to me as shaking my ass to 'Crazy in Love' by Beyoncé. I was confused by the dribbling element; quite often I'd be tricked by one of the lads' nimble foot play. Now I know foot play to be a whole different ball game. I remember being totally mindfucked when I learned that you don't toe punt a football and that to have more control you're supposed to use the instep of your foot. That seems a bit poofy to me.

I was useless in defence and I was useless as a striker . . . so they stuck me in the goal. No plot twist here: I was useless in the goal as well. That's actually where I broke my fingers, as one of the lads came charging down the pitch with a look of anger, eyeing up which corner they were going to shoot. I dove to the right, arms up like I was screaming the bridge of an S Club song, only to have my hand penetrated by the might of the ball, crashing ferociously against the goal post and fracturing my middle fingers in three places.

I tried. I failed. Football wasn't for me. My fingers are still wonky to this day and it's a nightmare to find a gorgeous ring that fits my deformed digits. I still have queer fear when I'm walking in a park and a kid's ball comes flying over, the kid jumping and beckoning for me to kick the ball back. I look so camp when I kick it back and quite often the little shit laughs at me. Little do they know I sucked off their dad.

At least it meant that I didn't have to pretend to be

interested in what the offside rule was. The anxiety I felt whenever that question popped up – and I still don't get it. Why don't they all just kick the ball into the goal?

Now, I'm athletic – enough. I can jump off a chair and slam my crotch into a split on the ground. I can defy gravity by doing shit like being a human flag on a pole. I can do crazy stuff with my body but this didn't really help me much in high school. I had to find what I enjoyed and work my arse off at it. For a lot of queer people, we aren't given that option at school. Physical education usually results in panic attacks or the feeling of a pulsing heart, sweaty palms and another forged letter or a twisted ankle. When I speak to a lot of queer people, they often relay the trauma they experienced from sports in school. I always found it confusing how we were allowed to mix 'boys and girls' when it came to activities such as cross-country running or rounders but I wasn't allowed to trade in rugby for netball. To be honest, I'd have loved to play rounders professionally. It gave me baseball vibes and I was always obsessed with American high schools. Naturally, I thought I was Hilary Duff in *Cinderella Story*, destined to marry Chad Michael Murray.

I've spoken about my attention-seeking tendencies. When it came to sports, even though I was rarely taken seriously, I would still give it my all. People would often say how 'surprised' they were that I would break the school record for cross-country running, or how I was actually pretty decent at most sports other than football. My body was naturally athletic, passed down from my dad's side (sorry, Mum). My grandmother was a dancer in the West End and my dad was a bodybuilder in the eighties. Some of the photos of my Dad are so ridiculously camp, posing in front of a Christmas tree in a tiny thong with a ripped six-pack and a cheeky smile. Fuck knows where I get it from.

I can't deny the negative impact that sports and toxic masculinity had on me as a kid. I was constantly made to feel inadequate, even though I really wasn't that bad. Whenever one of the captains would pick me first it would result in 'woos' from the other boys because, even though I wasn't out, everyone assumed I was a raging homosexual, so it was like the boys fancied me or something.

Funny story: I actually ended up sleeping with a few of those lads from high school, often receiving messages from some of them to this day, which I ignore now because I've moved past that fantasy, love myself more and now feel quite sorry for their fragile arses. Some of them would blackmail me into keeping quiet, telling me that if I told people then their family would seriously harm me. I think for a lot of naive queer people who may have experienced similar situations, there was a certain thrill to this. Like a dopamine hit, or an adrenaline rush. There was a feeling of doing something naughty and getting away with it. I usually did get away with it, but it's those hidden experiences that I've had to work hard to detach from. Never being made to feel like you're good enough, sexy, or wanted really does take a toll on you, no matter how innate your desire to seek attention may be. No wonder I started puffing the magic dragon.

Mainly we're taught that school sports and a student's participation in them brings about a sense of pride for the school community and helps with our physical health. I feel like for a lot of people under the LGBTQ+ umbrella, this simply ain't the case. Even though competitive sports in school didn't exactly bless me with the beginnings of a career as an Olympian, I went on to become East London's bendiest bitch and I would thank school sports a big fat zero!

I've mentioned earlier in the book that one of my biggest regrets was that I stopped dancing. It's true, I did, mainly because the transition between middle school and high school was so rough on me and it's taken me a lot of self-reflection to realise that it fucked me up. I always believed I was prepared for that jump. In middle school, despite being terrible at football, I was pretty much top at everything else. Running, gymnastics – hell, I was even one of the best in the school at long jump, despite not being blessed with legs up to my armpits.

Outside of school I would attend dance classes three times a week. I did everything from jazz, tap and modern to freestyle. Freestyle was my favourite. I went to two different dance teachers and they always pushed my potential until it came to having to conform to assigned gender roles. I hated that part of it. Estelle's dance company would take place on Wednesdays and Saturdays at the Hippodrome Circus and Esta's would take place at the Marina Centre in Great Yarmouth on a Tuesday evening. At both, it was just me and the girls. As I've said before, feminine energy was always around me – and not just at home. It got to the point where if I was forced to work with boys I found it exceedingly difficult, except for those few who turned out to be queer as well. It's like we have some sort of magnetic field, even when we're kids. Maybe it's like how dogs can see ghosts – kids can always see queers.

My grandmother was a dancer in the West End. Maggie. She passed away recently at the respectable age of 81. Maggie's last years weren't the easiest and she endured a lot of mental and physical problems, but her younger days sounded like a hoot. A tiller girl among other things, Maggie's dancing capabilities were phenomenal and those genes were passed down to me, I think. I often wonder what life would have been like if I had continued those classes.

At Esta's, I remember participating in a county championship for freestyle dancing, the one where all the girls would wear those stretchy bodysuits all the drag queens wear now, making everyone look like baton twirlers. I didn't wear them, sadly. I opted for tracksuit bottoms and those two-for-£10 T-shirts from Topman and a questionable hat. I wish I had been able to wear those dance costumes though. I probably would have had my own TV show or something . . .

When I was in year four, I entered the school talent show and performed possibly the most ridiculously heterosexual song an enby could choose – 'Hey Baby' by Bruce Channel. I remember the choreography even now, and bearing in mind I was about eight years old, it was . . . weirdly provocative. I did a lot of hip thrusts to the beat of 'Ooh, Ahh' and gyrated across the stage to the cheers of an assembly hall of Catholic teachers and students. Maybe my cute gap tooth and flaming red hair made the performance as innocent as I intended but whatever it was, it resulted in me winning the entire thing. Apparently, I won because everyone was blown away at my confidence. I was the only middle schooler to enter the talent show on their own. See, natural show-off.

I look back now and wish I had had the courage to continue being myself in high school, instead of getting caught up in drugs and trying to be popular. That desire to fit in faded very fast but by that point I was too old to rejoin any of the dance classes. Then I ended up at a sixth form which didn't have a dance class. Not only did high school mess up my psyche, it forced me to stop the only sport I actually enjoyed as a queerdo. I'm still triggered whenever I watch J. Lo music videos.

What I can really pass on to anyone reading this, no matter your age, is that it's never too late to do what you want to do. If you want to take up running, do it. If you want to become a hockey player, by all means pucker up. If you want to open an inclusive Quidditch club you have my full support. I have regrets and what-ifs about dancing and I don't want you to feel the same way. Maybe that's the reason I stopped, so that I could eventually tell others to do the opposite of me in a queer self-help book.

In my early twenties, after the years of partying and abusing my body and only taking it out for the odd run to compensate, I learned the benefits that exercise can have not only on my physical body, but my mental health

as well. It's astounding what regular exercise can do to help your positive mental attitude (PMA). And it's important for me to not sound like a wanker when I write this. Find what works for you. Don't be put off by sports in school. There are hundreds of different exercise classes you could join, no matter what level you're at. What lockdown has taught us is that there are a shit-tonne of online classes you can do to help muster up the confidence to join a real-life class. Realistically, if you're someone that doesn't exercise regularly, you might struggle at the beginning, but you'll reap the benefits after and you may even get slightly addicted to the burn.

Don't compare yourself to those around you. If you join a gym or class, stop looking at how everybody else looks and get lost in what you're doing. Putting on a podcast or your favourite playlist is gonna help you work harder. Try and enjoy yourself as much as possible as well – that's really important. You're taking time away from the stress of life.

I know how difficult this can be for a queer person. I've always felt like a sore thumb in the gym. Gyms would bring back memories of school and that toxic environment. Nobody looks like they're having fun in there. The grunting, the sportswear, the shifty looks. It's quite cruise-y to be honest. It reminds me of a time where I didn't love myself, and nobody wants to be reminded of that.

I've been fucked in many gyms across London, metaphorically speaking. I've got about six Gymbox towels in my house that I've held on to for keepsakes. I've been to more Fitness Firsts than Theresa May's been in wheat fields. I've been sniggered and jeered at, I've had fitness instructors laugh when I walk in wearing booty shorts and a crop top. I've had blokes in the changing room move away from me because they thought I wanted to get a look at their pecker. It's been a struggle as a non-binary person to navigate those spaces with confidence. It comes back to my need to always prove people wrong, fitness included. I'd annihilate any classes I did. I'd try everything, from animalistic classes that focused on body weight and primal moves to weighted yoga classes. I got a real kick out of showing people my body's capabilities. As a queer person, I unapologetically took up space in that heteronormative world and looked great while I did it, but this took a lot of balls (pardon the pun). They don't have people like me in mind when these spaces are created. Although if you look back at the eighties, fitness classes looked gayer than John Travolta.

Perhaps I was born in the wrong era, but I would give anything to go to a class led by Jane Fonda, where everyone wears spandex and accessorises their leotards with belts. Maybe I need to hit up my pal Lisa Rinna from

The Real Housewives of Beverly Hills and get her on it because we need an over-the-top fitness craze to take hold. Bring back the crop tops that the straight men would wear. I drool at the prospect.

I have a banging idea. It's that one day I'll be able to open up an inclusive fitness centre with a heavy focus on accessibility and queerness. I want it to be tacky but high-end, with my own Bimini's Booty Bonanza class blowing up across the globe. I envision the place being covered in disco balls, with Jodie Harsh DJing five nights a week and drag artists serving you some vegan energy protein drinks at the reception. I'd love a fitness space that was created free of toxic masculinity, where people could go hassle free and not experience wankers trying to either touch them up or bring them down. I think it's important for queers to have access to a fitness space they can feel comfortable and respected in. Instead of being laughed at, we're laughing at a joke Lawrence Chaney has just told on the mic in between Lisa Rinna's water aerobics and my booty class. I think it's totally doable. The only unrealistic part about this idea is the prospect of anyone laughing at a Lawrence Chaney joke.

Until this happens, find a space that makes you feel safe and go to it. Even find a fitness buddy to go with you. Someone that you can trust who will spur you on. I've manoeuvred my way through these spaces and I know they're enough to put anyone off, but we deserve to feel protected and able to use them. Avoid gyms that don't have a Pride flag up in June as well. That's usually a giveaway.

As queers, we should unlearn the conditioning that we might have attached to sports and fitness. When I worked on *Drag Race*, one of the producers (aptly nicknamed the Queen Handlers) was part of a female football team that was open to all women. They are super-inclusive and practise regularly. It's about empowering, uplifting and helping each other. A bonding experience with fitness benefits. Ooh la.

If this interests you, look up queer-friendly activities. I know lots of rowing clubs have an LGBTQ+ focus if that tickles your pickle. I'm sure there are groups for any sport and if there isn't, make one. Find like-minded people and create a badass queer darts team, if that's your thing. Not sure how fun darts is but I'm sure you could make it work. I believe in you, you sexy thing.

Personally, I found my queer-friendly fitness space in yoga. The things yoga can do to your body and mind should not be underestimated. I've experimented with all styles of yoga and I love them all. One of my favourite styles was hot yoga (not bikram, we don't mention that in the community) and that moment in savasana (the corpse pose at the end) is one of the best feelings ever. Once

you've sweated out all of the rage and regret, ugh, it's honestly orgasmic. I wouldn't class yoga as a sport though. You aren't meant to get competitive, although a lot of students do. I've taught a lot of yoga and you can see the ones that are getting a kick out of being better than others. I know we're not meant to, but I think humans are naturally competitive.

I first did yoga in the mountains north of Thailand, in a gorgeous little village called Pai. People often told me about the magic of Pai but to get there people often died. I know that makes it sound like this gruelling expedition but it's literally just a crazy mountain road that extends for three hours past Chiang Mai; because the roads were so old and rickety you'd hear horror stories of minibuses flying off the edge into a pit of death and doom.

Anyway, I didn't die. The journey was totally worth it, and when I arrived in Pai I could sense that the place was magical. The 'town centre', if you can call it that, is in the shape of an L. It has lots of little bars, restaurants and shops and a mix of tourists and local people. What I noticed quite quickly about Pai was the pace. It was slow in comparison to the big city (and even Great Yarmouth). People did what they wanted, when they wanted. After my infamous drug problem, this was exactly what I needed.

I rented a scooter and started driving around to find somewhere to stay. I had been recommended a hostel called The Circus and thought it sounded terribly fitting. It was all open-plan with these tiny little huts that back

then I called home. It had an infinity pool overlooking the lush green mountains. It was idyllic. In fact, I always said that I'd lock myself away in Pai to write my first book. That hasn't happened, but who knows, perhaps it will in the future.

Anyway, this is when I first took part in yoga. I'd obviously heard about yoga – I do live in East London – but had never practised it. Bearing in mind that Pai is much hotter than East London, we did sunset yoga. Now this is where things might start to sound a bit self-righteous, but I really felt connected to myself for the first time in a long time. I followed the movements with my breath, listened to the guidance of the teacher and realised I still had a lot of the mobility I had gained from dancing, which obviously made me enjoy the practice even more. Cut to my brain having flashes of me doing all of those difficult yoga poses with a scenic backdrop and an inspirational quote (if you can find evidence online of this, tweet me, because it's out there).

That was my first taste of yoga. I practised a couple more times but then travelled down south to do the typical backpackers' route. It's wild to think that this was six years ago. So much has changed in those years. (I just looked in the mirror and had a real *Death Becomes Her* moment then. What I lacked at 21 – SPF and moisturiser – I sure make up for now *Madeline Ashton smile*.)

I finished my travels through South East Asia with a longing to continue yoga practice. I didn't do it a lot in the south, I'll be honest. I actually spent the majority of the time on a little island called Koh Phi (made famous because of that famous All Saints song 'Pure Shores') and spent most of the time bucket-deep in SangSom. Not very spiritual.

When I returned home, I moved into a warehouse in north-east London. It wasn't the glamorous warehouse I always imagined I'd live in, you know, those downtown city ones you see on sitcoms as a kid. It was an over-priced tin but locally there were little pop-ups happening all over, which is how I ended up at a weekly yoga class on a Wednesday evening with my first ever teacher, Vanessa Joy. She was so lovely. It was a slow but intense hatha flow. People think if yoga is slow it means it isn't doing much to the body, but if you get your breath right you don't need a fast-paced flow to break a sweat.

I attended this class every Wednesday for about six months. I was practising elsewhere as well, for instance, by myself in the park. I was pushing my body further than the class allowed me, partly because I knew my body could do more and secondly because I'm a show-off. I was fully blossoming into my full-on hippy era. Really, I just needed a deep exfoliation and a hot bath. I dyed my beard – yes, I had a beard! – every colour possible. I was an eco-warrior at Boomtown. I worked at an incredible world music venue in Dalston (Passing Clouds, where I met Ella).

In hindsight, I think I was overcompensating slightly. The scales had tipped from one end to the other. I still always liked to get my body out and be a bit cheeky but when I see photos of this era, I do question a lot of the choices I made. Like why am I always wearing a rainbow?

Still, I had a lot of fun at that time, although I was back to smoking a lot of weed. I don't smoke it now, I can't. The weed that is accessible now – Skunk – is so strong. The devil's lettuce. But back then, I had my best friend living with me in the warehouse, I had graduated and had naivety and youth on my side. A bit of weed wasn't doing me any harm.

After graduating, I decided I wanted to go back out and see the world so I researched where I could do a yoga retreat. That's when I came across some teacher training courses and thought, fuck it, why not? I was looking to expand my practice so this seemed the right move, whether I was going to share the practice or not. The schedule looked intense but I like a challenge. I booked my place, got my flights and it was goodbye London, hello *Eat Pray Love*. Twenty-eight days of yoga, with four days off throughout that. I was nervous about the daily wake-up time (4.30am). I'd only ever seen 4:30am on the other side of the coin so this was going to be a new experience. See what I mean about sliding scales?

I arrived at Delhi airport and it was positively chaotic. I made my way up to the north of India to Rishikesh, a spiritual city on the Himalayan mountains. It's the birthplace of yoga, where the ancient practice was first founded. I felt like I wanted to experiment authentically so that's where I went.

Rishikesh is gorgeous but what I discovered was just how much the place catered for Western folk like me.

A lot of the travellers looked like me and I sensed that they were seeking something, like me. That isn't necessarily a bad thing and hey, I'm part of that. I struggled to find a teacher-training course that seemed authentic among the hundreds in Rishikesh. And yes, I do understand the privilege that comes from my white arse travelling to India and paying a lot of money to seek this authenticity, but I was enrolled and ready to give it a bloody good go.

I think I was searching for all the answers during my yoga training but what I learned is that spirit doesn't come naturally. You have to seek it. In Rishikesh it was promised everywhere but I found that not necessarily to be true. I wouldn't say I had a bad time but I think I overestimated my reasons for going. I did have a great time though, it was just eye-opening in some places.

Each day was set up pretty much the same. We'd be woken up super-early, mostly to the sounds of monkeys jumping around. It did feel pretty mystical to wake up in the Himalayan mountains. The city of Rishikesh is viewed as a holy city in India, meaning you can't drink alcohol. I'm pretty sure there were some places that did sneak some booze in, but I was looking forward to being away from London and abstaining from any naughty influences. I was ready for my body to be reborn. We'd do a two-hour hatha practice followed by breakfast. I was vegan, obviously, but in India a vegan diet is pretty easy to come by. We'd then have a bit of free time before we got on with the more theoretical based parts of the study, including anatomy, philosophy and history. We'd also do a 'doctor' class where we'd focus on one yoga pose and dissect it to great lengths. The evenings would end with a two-hour ashtanga practice, followed by meditation. Our meditation teacher was the same as our philosophy teacher and whether he was a great actor or just the real deal, he seemed to be the most authentic person I'd met yet. It made me feel exhilarated.

However, it was meditation that I found the most difficult. I live in London; we never take time out for ourselves, do we? I love the bustle of constantly being on-the-go, so spending an hour each evening trying to shut my thoughts down seemed impossible. We were told to start the beginning of this meditative journey lying down and gradually as the course went on we would try to do it seated. The way meditation works is better with a straight spine because it allows the energy to flow around your body. The swami would guide us and occasionally you'd hear the odd snore coming from a student who had dozed off. (I never did, thankfully.) I did start to get better at it as the days passed. We would be told to focus our gaze (with eyes closed) at the 'third eye' or pineal gland. I will say I did start to experience colourful visuals and vibrations but maybe I was tripping again. I did feel lovely after meditation. Very serene – an unfamiliar feeling.

Fast-forward to about a third of the way through the training, and I was starting to get slightly fidgety. I'm unsure whether it's my ignorant Britishness but I've always tried to question everything. I started to notice cracks in parts of the philosophy we were taught. In no way am I disregarding the art of yoga in any way because

I love it, and I believe the teachings to have pure intentions. Maybe it was just the guru we had but a few things didn't add up. We were told that we should have love and respect for all sentient beings. Don't harm another living being. I mean, I already adopt that approach as much as I can. Then in Ayurvedic practice, which is more of a food-lifestyle approach to diet, we were told about certain dairy and meat products that we were able to eat. When I asked what the correlation between these was, as someone that was already vegan, I was kind of ushered to be quiet. I protested, saying I didn't get how the yoga practice tells us to not harm other living beings but that we can eat them. It was that moment I was told that I wasn't ready and that it wasn't my time.

I was told I wasn't ready because I questioned them on an aspect I was genuinely wanting to understand. Obviously, it doesn't make much sense on paper but in front of an entire class of students hearing those words kinda hurt. Anyway after that interaction I started to notice other flaws in the philosophy. To me, it didn't gel well with what I viewed the practice of yoga to be. It's all someone's interpretation at that moment anyway, but I started to become a bit more aware instead of walking around with rose-tinted glasses. Maybe he was right and I wasn't ready or maybe I was resisting being part of a cult.

What I realised in Rishikesh was that there was an abundance of training places. What was once a holy city had become a capitalist yoga haven, which didn't sit well with me either. I'm glad I went and trained there because it wouldn't have felt right learning anywhere else. I also met some phenomenal people, including some who had also begun to question parts of the training. I tried my hardest not to be negative because I didn't want to tarnish mine or anyone else's experience but it reassured me that I wasn't being stupid.

There were quite large numbers of Western people, predominantly women, that I'd see walking side by side with a guru, wearing traditional Hindi garments and bindis. I spoke to some who seemed to have their eyes glazed over, as if they were under some sort of trance. I learned that a lot of people ended up giving their lives up and staying over here longer to learn deeper teachings. More likely than not, they had experienced a form of abuse, trauma or addiction that resulted in them seeking a higher power, similar to why I was out there. We all shared a feeling of wanting to believe that this life is more than what it says on the tin but perhaps never feeling that any organised religion we had been taught resonated with us.

People were lost and wanted approval. That's no bad thing but I think there were a few instances where some exploitation of weakness was occurring. I took it upon myself to enjoy the rest of the experience and to take from it all I could in an attempt to further my own spiritual learning.

My entire trip to India was reflective. I realised that in order to find what I was looking for I had to focus on myself and what I wanted. I worked out that the only person that would make me feel like a bad bitch was me, myself and I. My yoga practice deepened and I certainly learned a lot. I learned to be open, more aware of what's going on and to follow my own intuition. It strengthened my beliefs and it was an otherworldly experience, flaws aside. Even diamonds have flaws *insert *Real Housewives* quote here*.

Life Lesson 9:
Have a PMA

We were deep into the third full lockdown in the UK when *Drag Race* was airing. That entire experience got off to a furiously stressful start because all of us wanted to be out in the bars and the clubs, doing screenings and being surrounded by other queers. *Drag Race* is a bit like football for queers but I'm sure if we had broken the rules and congregated in our thousands to watch it the government would have acted. Maybe they'd have let it slide if we were all waving the flag of St George. Regardless, the experience as the episodes aired each week often brought on spurts of anxiety for me about how I would be perceived, what I said this week, or who I slagged off that week. I was pretty lovely to everyone except when I said, 'I don't know you love' to Veronica. Honestly, that played on my mind because it was a bit bitchy for my taste. I think I was hungover from that confessional.

That particular lockdown was the most difficult for everybody, I think. I know it was for my household in particular. As it was January and February, infamously the worst months for desolate and bleak weather, everyone was having a pretty rubbish time. It didn't have the same energy as the first lockdown because I didn't have the pressure of the show. We had also been living in a house with a moderately adequate garden and so luckily had been able to enjoy the gorgeous sunshine and blue skies. I won't bore you with details about the weather despite it being a mandatory British trait, but it did help first time round. We all had a real sense of camaraderie at home and online. We were in this together. We had each other's backs.

The winter lockdown wasn't like that. We all hated each other by that point; everyone was sick of Boris doing those rubbish updates where he mumbled through a pre-written speech and was about as personable as a cactus dildo. Everybody seemed a lot sadder, particularly in the area I live in in London. It's not that far from Stoke Newington, but when you cross into Stamford Hill/Seven Sisters you see a huge difference in poverty and class.

The first two episodes I was having kittens before the premiere. I knew that tape gate happened in episode one, balloon gate in episode two, and I also felt incredibly nervous about the portrayal of Princess Julia. She's my gay icon, regardless of what the judges said. I have huge respect for her and felt sick with nerves about how it was going to play out on the show. When I saw the video of her reaction it eradicated any negative feelings I had towards it. It was the purest reaction to the situation and she was overwhelmed by it. It was exactly why I did it. She deserves to be celebrated for all that she has done over the years for our community. Selflessly.

Then episode five happened and the now culturally significant hit single 'UK Hun?' broke on to our screens and since then I basically haven't stopped working. That was when we returned from lockdown and people could see I had a fire lit under my booty. I was hungry while all these other girls were thirsty. I'd had time to reflect and I was ready to show the world what I was capable of. Is this what success looks like? Maybe in the eyes of heteronormative capitalism, but I found that I was sacrificing my personal wellbeing by constantly working. It's that toxic productivity that I mentioned in previous chapters. I'll talk about why I haven't yet learned to say no later on in this chapter, but you can probably guess it's deeply rooted in being a queer suddenly thrust into the public eye.

As my following increased, so did the amount of support and love from the fandom. Even with my minor slip-ups early on I didn't receive any Bimini Bon Backlash. I don't read every single comment so I might be lying about that, but from what I did read, it was bloody lovely.

I noticed the shift when I said, 'You just gotta have a PMA' to Lawrence and it somehow became a meme. I actually signed a person's arm at one of my gigs recently and they got PMA in my handwriting tattooed on their body. A moment. The run started to go smoothly and I was overwhelmed by the amount of love I was being shown. And that seriously helps to fuel a PMA.

We filmed the final episode a few weeks before you all watched it so I knew who the finalists were and who could possibly snatch the crown. There was a lot of championing for me to win but all I ever wanted was to make it to the final. I'm a big believer in manifesting and that's what I manifested constantly. When Lawrence, a deserving winner, took the tiara it was something that had always been part of their plan, their dream. They are also super-talented. I don't think myself or Tayce wanted it as much as Lawrence so I was overjoyed when they announced they had won. Like, genuinely happy. We were filming a private screening with the four finalists and one guest (my mum) didn't take it quite as graciously as me, but that was because she was about three Bacardis deep. I love her a lot but I had to keep reminding her that it was okay. I think she fed into the hype around me winning way more than I did.

Not winning has been a blessing. I've had some of

the most mind-blowing things offered to me. I did my own editorial for *Italian Vogue*. That's mental to me. There was a lot of backlash when I didn't win but I felt this was at the expense and discredit of Lawrence and all the work they put in. It's delightful to be supported but I hate any form of bullying or viciousness and the fans know I'm not about that. I didn't argue with anyone on the show. I was dancing around telling everyone to have a positive mental attitude. I'm too old for the drama (although my skin is getting younger every day).

I'm a competitive person but I also know that I did the best I could. They had the opportunity to crown me . . . but it wouldn't have been punk to win anyway.

The Queerness of Failure

If you're reading this and you're queer, you have probably experienced a lot of feelings of inadequacy and often felt like you're not enough because of the constraints put on us by society. This is a pretty standard part of

growing up as a queer person because you're not able to start truly living your life until you find out who you are and gain the confidence to live authentically as yourself. I've spoken about how I struggled to fulfil expected gender norms growing up, which I think led to a lot of the feelings of failure I experienced over the years.

Lesbians, gay men and bi people realise they are 'failing' at the expectations of who they should desire. Queer and trans people often fail at being 'men' or 'women' and – as mentioned in earlier chapters – are often policed for their failings from a young age. This idea of being a 'gender failure' is something many LGBTQ+ people feel and something writers like Kate Bornstein have discussed at length in their works. But there is a freedom in knowing that we only 'fail' because the patriarchy has gaslit us into thinking there's a right way. As Bornstein writes: 'Let's stop pretending that we have all the answers, because when it comes to gender, none of us is fucking omniscient.' Hear hear!

I quit dancing before I came out as queer. I think that was one of the first moments that I felt like I was failing at life, because I'd get bullied or laughed at for doing what I enjoyed. Then when I wasn't able to get down with what other teen lads were doing, I also felt like a failure. This probably has something to do with why I started smoking weed so young; it was a coping mechanism to make me forget those feelings. We know that it's called repression and repression isn't good, or at least that's what my therapist would say if I went to one. (If you really want to dig deep into your psyche and question your life choices, I'd recommend writing a book. It's like therapy, only harder.)

I remember being at school and having a 'successful' version of my life set out for me. You're constantly told you need to get good grades to go on to college, then university, then get a cushty little money earner, get a mortgage, get married to a single partner, save for a pension and then retire after being the ideal candidate for citizen of the year. If you have the opportunity to work your way up the ladder and start earning more money you're seen as successful. Mostly, the successful people we looked up to didn't represent a lot of the queer community. I never saw anyone else like me on the morning news or even high up in journalistic positions. I felt like a failure because I didn't go on to become a journalist after studying for three years. A huge part of that came down to ethics and not wanting to sell my soul and write about shit that I didn't want to write about. We all know the dark side of the media, especially in the UK.

I'm a big believer that we can all achieve great things if we put our minds to it. But I'm also aware that there are many factors that can prevent this, like our educational, economic and social conditions. Jack Halberstam wrote a book called *The Queer Art of Failure*, in which he argues that failure is a defining experience of queerness. Jack discusses finding alternatives to the way we view success. We mainly view success through a capitalist and heteronormative lens. He discusses the idea of 'low theory', which outlines a disposition, or willingness, for us queer people to fail and to lose our way rather than embrace society's normative notions of success – something I have experienced throughout the years. The idea of success is highly capitalistic. That's why all of the people that are running the country went to the same private schools. They usually come from a wealthy background and their idea of having fun was burning fifty-pound notes in front of homeless people.

In *The Queer Art of Failure*, Halberstam says, 'Queerness offers the promise of failure as a way of life . . . but it is up to us whether we choose to make good on that promise in a way that makes a detour around the usual markers of accomplishment and satisfaction.'

Quite a few people who identify as LGBTQ+ attempt to follow the path set out for them by society. I know people that work the system to their advantage without facing too many repercussions. It isn't impossible to work that way and it can hugely benefit some people. For a lot of my peers, myself included, this way of life didn't come as organically. When I worked for a big advertising agency, we didn't have a uniform but we would have to dress relatively smart. I struggled with not being able to turn up to the office every day in clothes that allowed me to express my identity and I endured a feeling of imposter syndrome the whole time I worked there. It was awful. I felt like I had failed at what was expected of me and that's why I quit to work as a yoga instructor and was a really awful drag queen for about 18 months – until I watched a YouTube tutorial about how to do a smoky eye. The rest was history.

I do still feel imposter syndrome. I'm not going to ask

for sympathy and I'm not trying to say, 'woe is me', because my life has changed so drastically over the last few months, in a positive way. I'm now in situations I never expected, and sometimes I do feel I don't belong. When I'm filming a TV show with a mainly heteronormative audience and panel, I get nervous that it's all going to be ripped away from underneath me. I think I've worked every single day because I'm getting a taste of mainstream success in sectors that aren't filled with queer people, so I have to work twice as hard not to fuck it up. It's pretty radical that I'm the first queen from *Drag Race* to have their own editorial and feature in *Vogue*, other than RuPaul herself. I'm constantly worried I'm gonna fuck all of this up and it has led me to have bursts of anxiety. I have to remind myself sometimes that I'm not a robot and that I am human. We have to give ourselves a bloody day off now and then.

Let's be honest, the playing field has never been level for queer people. Not all is lost, though, as we are seeing increasing mainstream representation. Think about Lil Nas X, a Black gay rapper who is at the height of mainstream culture and being unapologetically sexual and queer. It's inspiring to see him performing at the BET awards and kissing another male on stage in a culture that is usually quite homophobic. I'm like yas! queen.

During one episode of the show, when Lawrence and I were putting our slap on, we spoke about lockdown and what we had both gotten up to. I mentioned earlier that the first lockdown was the easier one for me, even though I had stopped filming and had no income.

Lawrence didn't experience this, and although they lived with their friend, all of their work also dried up. It showed a very vulnerable side of our community and the work we do, tossed to the side and forgotten about. It made a lot of us queer people feel pretty redundant. Lawrence opened up about their struggles, particularly when they were witnessing a lot of the country reopen for events during the summer and Scotland remained closed. That's when they said 'Get fucked' to my blabbing on about having a PMA.

The truth is, they're right – it's hard to keep a positive mental attitude. For a lot of us queens, it was easy to fall into a negative headspace. Not being able to work and feeling quite helpless, combined with not being able to meet up with people for sex or see your partner (I wasn't able to see my boyfriend for many months because we did in fact follow the rules ... unlike some senior officials), and not being able to go to parties and interact with other queer people was hard. Imagine how difficult it must have been for trans people who were already on long waiting lists for healthcare to find out that their wait was about to become *even* longer. All of these things became increasingly difficult to deal with and there have been many lives lost due to the neglect of trans healthcare. It's tragic and heartbreaking that healthcare for a trans person has become so politicised that it's resulting in trans people taking their own lives. I often wonder how detrimental to who I am today it would have been to spend a whole year not being around queer people and being in a form of solitary confinement when I first moved to London.

What I was grateful for were the friends who surrounded me during the pandemic. Even though we had no idea how long it was going to last and walking to the shop looked like a scene from *The Handmaid's Tale*, we had each other and it helped to stay positive. We'd exercise, dance around, read and sunbathe in the garden. We also played a lot of cards and had a lot of laughs. I'm lucky because not everyone had that, but it did help me keep a positive mindset. I also decided to buy a 12-quid chair from Argos and teach myself to do some gravity-defying chair stunts. That was fun.

I try to stay positive as much as possible. I've said it before: it isn't easy and it isn't every day that I do a Cher Lloyd and hop out of bed and turn my swag on. The pandemic taught me who and what was important in life and that our wellbeing and that of our friends should be our ultimate focus.

The Benefits of Failure

As difficult as it can be to get your head around the feeling of failure, you have to try and think about the benefits it can have. I think I'm probably exempt from having a midlife crisis because I've already fucked up so many times and I've been able to learn ways to handle those situations.

It's important to view success on non-binary terms. It is a matter of degree and if we believe success to be this binary concept it's likely going to negatively impact our

efforts, happiness and what we want to achieve. Instead of constantly comparing ourselves to others, in a world where social media rules our lives, we have to avoid seeing ourselves as failures if we don't qualify for success in society's terms. If we think of success in those binary terms, what does it actually constitute? I was watching *Keeping Up With The Kardashians* recently. They have become the pinnacle of what young people look up to. They are all successful businesswomen, creating multi-billion-dollar empires and on a superficial level, they seem to have it all. In the episode, Kim discussed her marriage breakdown. She talked about her heartbreak and said all she wants is to be happy and have a chilled life with her partner. She is the epitome of how we view success yet she doesn't feel fulfilled in her soul. What we measure success against shouldn't be binary.

For queers who don't often get or have access to the same opportunities in life, we need to break down the binary of individual success and individual failure, find alternatives to these conventional markers, and think of different ways to relate to one another.

If we view people as either a failure or a success, it's

quite easy to set standards for how we view 'success' to be, and if we don't meet that standard then we can easily class ourselves as failures.

I mentioned earlier that I'd been quite fortunate with the fandom and 'stan culture' surrounding *Drag Race*. I wish it was the same for all of my season sisters, but as I'm quite close to A'Whora I witnessed the abuse she was getting on social media. Some of the names people would call her were abhorrent and totally uncalled for. When people say nasty things about us, we quite often take that to heart and it makes us feel like we've failed. I remember reading the comments section once on my photo and even though there were hundreds of positive comments, I only saw the one negative and it stuck with me. Negativity breeds negativity; if I allowed myself to get wrapped up in it, it would be detrimental to my being. Sister did an article for the *Guardian* where they spoke about their experience during the show and the abuse they received, even as far as death threats. This counteracts what the show is supposed to be about – a fun and uplifting celebration of queer culture. When I read Sister's article, titled 'One troll described how he'd like to see me die', it really shone a light on a toxic side of pop culture, one that we've seen tear down other successful people.

That's why when it came to the final with myself, Tayce and Lawrence it was important for me to constantly uplift my sisters. We'd been through a global pandemic and filmed arguably one of the best seasons of *Drag Race* ever and I felt like we had connected on a deeper level because of this. I made it very clear to the people that supported me not to bring the others down because it doesn't build me up. It hasn't been the easiest period for us all and I try my hardest to spread as much love as possible. (That's why I was promiscuous in my early twenties. A lot of people deserved my love.)

During the second part of filming, I went back and tried to detach myself from the competitive side I had and focus on doing the remainder of the show for myself. I didn't see the others as competitors because they were all shit. (Kidding.) I decided to focus on competing with myself and myself only. It really helped me put my all into everything. I'd only done stand-up once before and it was in a safe space. Doing stand-up to Ru, Michelle, Dawn French and Alan Carr didn't feel like a safe space, especially when we had no audience. That was torture. I went back and didn't take it so seriously, which is important.

In *The Queer Art of Failure* Halberstam writes: 'Being taken seriously means missing out on the chance to be frivolous, promiscuous, and irrelevant.' Once you embrace the idea that competition and individual success aren't all there is to life, you create new space for ways of relating to other people and understanding yourself. Look at all of the nonconformists over the years. They created their own lanes and did exactly what they wanted to do. It's about being receptive to the fact that you aren't always going to be perfect because perfection doesn't exist.

Nobody is perfect, and I'm nobody so that means I'm perfect. Can you remember when everyone had that as their username?

Imagine a world where we are less focused on individual success and are able to embrace the possibility of failure. If we stop striving for unattainable goals that exhaust our wellbeing, we can start to uplift others. And a side effect of uplifting others is that it helps to uplift you. Imagine the feeling you get when you make a gift for a friend and the reaction you get when you give it to them. Now imagine having that feeling every single day. It's important that we try and spread kindness to others. Compliment people. Support your friends when they feel like they've messed up. If we can spend time unifying, ultimately we can progress our mutual consciousness into a more open, loving society. Just as gender is a construct, so is success. Basically, we need to embrace the values of socialism, which, despite the capitalistic fantasy fed to the working class, would benefit us all. In basic terms, socialism is an economic and political system where the means of production, distribution and exchange are owned by the community. Our society is currently run under capitalism where the wealth gap is slowly increasing. Under capitalism, the worker is expendable because there will always be another person they are able to hire.

If we had affordable social housing instead of landlords buying up everywhere in London, we'd all be happier and more stable. I lived in a warehouse, which was originally full of artists living cheaply until it became desirable and trendy. The warehouse community was owned by the same family who would be making a tonne of money each month from all of the tenants. They did the bare minimum, the place was always filthy and I'm pretty sure I had asbestos on my ceiling but they were able to get away with it because the warehouse was slightly cheaper than a house and was easy to rent. Nobody asked for references.

If we properly invested in the NHS, access to healthcare would be easier and more manageable for the hardworking people that run our health system. It isn't the government that put the work in, it's the staff because they've dedicated their lives to the practice of healthcare and have to make it work in any way possible. Call me crazy but investing in the NHS, especially in mental health and transgender specialists, would save *a lot* of lives.

The school system sets you up for failure as well. Instead of being pushed into areas we excel at we're forced to study 11–13 different subjects and take exams in all of them. If schools focused less on assessments and exams then kids from disadvantaged backgrounds would have a better chance of learning properly and thriving. I don't know why socialism is seen as such a radical alternative to capitalism, which is just a failed system for the majority of its workers and creates such a divide in class, social politics and wealth.

Consider Dolly Parton. She may have written a song about the trials and tribulations of working 9 to 5, stumbling out of bed into the kitchen to pour yourself a cup of ambition and sticking it to the man, but as one of the world's most successful, and smartest, artists she has used her wealth and fame to give back. She created Dollywood to give her local community a boost for their economy. I'm yet to go but it's on my bucket list. She funds library books for children in London and does that amazing storytime with Dolly Parton, which is as iconic as it is camp. She only went and funded the Moderna vaccine as well, using her wealth to benefit the world. When I talk about having a PMA, she's pretty much the embodiment of it. She tries to share positivity with the world and uses her success to benefit others. That's what it's all about and you can do it while looking as fabulous as Dolly does every day. Long live the peroxide bimbos of the world that go against what society expects.

It's imperative for me to use the platform I've been given to spread love, elevate others and use my voice whenever possible. I was lucky enough to be asked to speak at London Trans Pride in the summer of 2021. The air was magical, the turnout was so heart-warming, and it was incredible to see the thousands of people descending through the streets of central London to support trans lives, with a heavy focus on healthcare and the unprecedented attacks on trans people, whether in the media or on the streets. I was nervous when I spoke because I'd never spoken at a protest or Pride event but listening to the speeches before and after me spurred me on to get up on the mic and stick my two cents in.

Whenever I create a line-up for an event I do myself, I want it to be as inclusive as possible. I'm lucky as hell with everything that's happened so far but if I did everything for my own personal gain, I think it'd make me feel shit. I've spoken about the vibrancy of the scene I'm from and I think every single artist that gets up on a stage deserves to take up space and get the same opportunities I'm given as a non-binary person. Never in a million years did I think I would have graced the cover of four magazines in a month, shoot for *Italian Vogue* and Calvin Klein, have the freedom and creativity to write and record my own music and even write my own book. I need a day of reflection, to get excited about all that has happened and how my life has changed but also how I can use this to benefit the lives of those who haven't been given the same opportunities I have.

Maybe failure is more us queers' style, and that's cool. That's the first step to having a positive mental attitude. Letting go, being silly, embracing failure, not taking life at face value or yourself too seriously. When we are able to admit to ourselves that some of our lifestyle choices are going to piss people off, it makes us happier and gives us a sense of relief. When we apply this to all areas of our life it's going to restore that PMA.

In the words of a person who has fully embraced the art of being a failure . . . 'the nipples are the eyes of the face'.

Life Lesson 10:
Release the Beast

Throughout the process of writing these pages, I've repeatedly asked myself ... why am I writing a book? What exactly do I hope people will take away from my story? Am I the non-binary answer to Carrie Bradshaw?

This book isn't necessarily intended as my memoir. I'm still 18, mentally. Sure, I've spoken about my life, but it wasn't my whole life story. I'm confident that will come later, hopefully in a few decades. It's practically, or impractically, my life story around gender and my experiences as a queer kid becoming a queer adult (admittedly, thanks to modern science and few sharp pricks I have the skin of an infant). In the process of distilling the lessons I've learned through my queer journey, I think the most significant message I wanted to get across to you all is that even though gender, queerness, family and

community may all be confusing as hell, being kind to yourself and others, above all else, is crucial.

Whether you're an ally to the community as a cis person, or you're on a journey of profound gender discovery, I hope that my words have given you some pearls of wisdumb to think about and resolved some of your questions. I also hope this book has got you asking plenty more.

I've spoken a lot about my own experience of gender, and writing this book has frankly been quite therapeutic for me. I'm 28 years old, studied a degree in journalism, didn't complete a masters in human rights, travelled numerous continents, took too many drugs, made lots of friends, lost lots of friends, battled my own addiction demons, had an out-of-body experience on ketamine, taught people the joy of yoga and then went on to a hit reality TV show to compete as a drag artist, all while figuring out who the hell I am and what I want to get out of this life. If you're one of those people that cut to the back of a book to find out the end, long story short, I've fucked up many times and that's okay. We all aim for perfection but it doesn't exist. You might look at my well-curated social media and the way I perform on stage and think I'm the most confident person ever, but a lot of the time I'm just making it up as I go along. I'd love to say I knew what I was doing the whole time, but really, I'm just putting my trust into a higher power and hoping for the best, basically.

The universe, god, Mother Nature, Oprah: whoever it is you might want to put your faith in, they've certainly helped me along the way. To be honest, I'm convinced that if a god did exist, they'd be non-binary. If only that had been represented in the stories of faith we'd been told in school, it would have made life a lot easier. Or if god came down and decided they were gonna enter Eurovision. Think about it though, surely god is genderless? God can be neither male or female. Perhaps god would be both, or neither. I'm sure if the belief in a genderless god arose now it would be ridiculed and laughed at because gender is political and profitable and I'm confident the magisterium of the Catholic Church doesn't want to deconstruct gender norms. If god is this all-seeing, all-being energy, they must be non-binary. They must exist beyond gender. It's the way I perceive it but I don't mean to compare myself to any god. Maybe an androgynous archangel, but not god. I truly believe that for our consciousness as a species to fully evolve we need to move past the insistence on a fixed gender binary, or at least have respect for everyone's different human experiences. How bloody boring would it be if we all did the same shit.

The conversation around gender will continue to change, and I'm excited for it. With more mainstream artists coming out as non-binary, there is hope for a future that embraces and celebrates uniqueness rather than feeling threatened by it. The way we think about gender is changing so rapidly. I feel like the rhetoric surrounding it is finally catching up with how I've constantly felt and offering me the language to discuss it now. My views on gender are my own. There are lots of incredible theorists on gender and I've included a reading list at

the end of the book. Go and read books on gender until you're sick of the word gender. The most valuable idea to take away from all of this is that gender isn't restrictive and it can change and fluctuate over time. Like the wind, or Katie Hopkins' career. It isn't permanent.

It may not be permanent or fixed, but currently gender *is* everywhere. It's in the form of systems and structures of oppression and also in our personal identity. There will inevitably be people who disagree with what I might define or claim as gender, and that's fine. It's – for better or worse – an ongoing sociological debate. I know there is often no point arguing with a person over their binary view of gender because it's something deeply treasured by many people and I try to look for common ground instead. I pray that by displaying my own tolerance of heteronormative ideas and ways of living, they'll reciprocate and offer me the same respect. If the lads from back home think it's outrageous that I wear a skirt, they're likely a lost cause to my gender enlightenment teachings, and perhaps need to have their mind expanded by a queer-baiting pop star wearing a feather boa on a red carpet . . .

I want the world to open up to the experiences of gender diversity rather than wasting time trying to repress them, you know, instead of stopping climate change or something. Actual plot twist: us gender benders ain't going anywhere.

You may have first-hand experience of the limitations that gender imposes on us all and how damaging the reinforcement of gender norms can be. It shouldn't be

ignored that quite often within my own LGBTQ+ community there is a sense that there's only 'one way' to be trans or non-binary and this always constrains people. This completely false narrative makes people think they have to look or be a certain way. I've experienced feelings of shame myself for not being queer or femme enough. This idea of 'passing' and needing to look as femme as possible often gives more power to a toxic form of masculinity, suggesting that gaining the acceptance of straight cis men is why we perform everything and present the way we do.

Sometimes, when certain groups of people feel like their own experience in society isn't progressing in the way they believe it should be, they begin to denounce people within their own community. Those targeted are often more disadvantaged individuals who rely on the wider community for mutual support and allyship. For example, the LGB Alliance believe they need to discard the T from the LGBTQ+ umbrella and that transgender people are holding them back from achieving genuine equality. Instead of going for the people in our society who uphold the dominant norms, they are closing the door behind them on a marginalised group IN OUR COMMUNITY. The mind boggles. Really, we should all be blaming patriarchal capitalism for creating the current conditions of the world, the gender binary, and everything else that's truly hindering equality, but go off.

One of Judith Butler's theories about gender is that we're constantly performing it. Gender only becomes comfortable because we've repeated gendered acts so often and therefore it feels 'real'. Queer people who deviate from the normative standards for gender performance are seen as failures by society and so don't expect the same opportunities or experiences as heterosexual, cisgender people, particularly those of us who came out or realised they were queer at a young age. Ultimately, this feeling can hugely influence a lot of the ways we feel and act throughout our lives. The world has been set up to make gender performance an ingrained and integral part of our everyday lives, which is why it's so difficult for us to not conform and perform otherwise. This is why I get 'faggot' shouted at me when I strut down Seven Sisters station in a tartan mini skirt and a gorgeous Lamoda heeled boot. I am not, per se, a 'faggot', but the mainstream idea about people who deviate from gender norms is still lagging so far behind that this is what the majority of people assume when they see me. I'm actually dead forward-thinking, me. What I'm trying to say is, forget the real/fake binary of gender. You don't have to be 'passable' to be trans, unless you want to look that way. If you're non-binary, there isn't a way of looking more or less non-binary. It's all about our personal experience. I know I keep saying that, but it's true. No gender is more real or authentic than another. We're always performing something anyway. Basically, we're all two-faced and we should just admit to it.

In the name of all non-binary gods, that got quite deep. I don't want you to feel any sympathy for me for being shouted at in the street. Chances are, I could give them a little slap and tickle if I absolutely wanted to.

I think what's so confusing about me for some people is that I look deliciously feminine but also have a really bloke-like rasp to my voice. I think it's great. I enjoy the juxtaposition. I can sound like Keith Flint but look like Pammy Anderson. The best of both worlds!

Let's talk about the fluidity of gender. I'm going to start by asking you a question. How often have you seen a blanket assumption about your assigned gender and thought, 'that doesn't resonate with me'? Go on . . . what pisses you off the most when this happens? Is it being told you can't be strong or that you can't cry? These are basic gender stereotypes that we know aren't true. Having a rigid binary upholds these false ideas. I can think of tonnes of examples . . . like the fact that I was meant to

be good at football because I had balls, or that when dancing I was expected to take the masculine role even though I was so obviously the opposite of that. We've seen and accepted how gender expectations have shifted over the years. You'd likely slap someone today if they said, 'go make me a sandwich, woman,' because aside from being an outrageously sexist request, what if you just don't want to make someone a fucking sandwich? What if you're not a bread artisan and think sourdough is shit? Go and make your own fucking sandwich, mate! Throughout time, we've seen some great women and men defy societal norms and go against the grain. Accepting non-binary values and identities isn't a new request. It's the next logical step in shifting our consciousness and creating a more tolerable, open world.

The way I relate myself to masculinity and femininity is always changing. Like I said in the fitness chapter, I would go to fitness classes and make sure I proved the teacher wrong because I *was* strong, even though I looked queer. Where we position ourselves on the gender spectrum can be forever fluctuating and changes to the ways we physically present ourselves to the world, sadly, will influence how the world reads and treats us. During the course of our lives, we might be neither, both, between, under, over, or beyond the binary altogether – and that's okay!

Gender is both personal and political. As much as our gender is our own and should always be viewed as a personal matter, we can't ignore the fact that it's also social and cultural. The reason I'm writing this book is political. I went on a reality television show that has been broadcast since 2009 and in 2021 a conversation around my personal identity was shown to millions of people. I was inundated with messages from people thanking me for my words (which, by the way, I'm so grateful for) but I was also slightly surprised that it was as impactful as it was. I never imagined my own personal views on gender and my own experiences would have such a moment and resonate with so many. I think it broke down a certain view of what being non-binary or gender nonconforming means. We're not all mullet-bearing, Yungblud-listening teenagers (we're mullet-wearing, Yungblud-listening twenty-somethings). I jest. What really happened was it broke down a certain view of what it means to be the kind of person we're only used to debating or discussing in theory. People saw an authentic, human portrayal of two non-binary experiences that didn't match the mainstream political stereotype of a 'gender traitor' or a 'woman hater'. Rather than seeing an entire group of people through a critical lens, we must think about the individual's personal experiences, try and connect with them and see them for who they are; complex, multifaceted humans.

Remember when L'Oréal infamously dropped Munroe Bergdorf three days after hiring her as their first transgender model for saying, 'all white people are complicit in racism'? It was deemed 'controversial' but for most of the so-called 'woke' generation that understood it, she wasn't wrong. We must look at all the different ways that oppressive systems and structures shape the behaviours and experiences of a person or group. If you say, 'not all white people are racist' because you're white

and feel you personally aren't racist, you neglect to reflect on the real system of power you might be unknowingly benefitting from – and complicit in – that disadvantages people of colour. As a white non-bine harvester, I also acknowledge that gender isn't all we should talk about. It can't be separated from the intersections of race, sexuality, class or disability; we should always focus on and consider all of these aspects of discrimination.

Gender being both personal and political is a tricky idea to navigate because either way you can't really win. If we see the patriarchy as including all men, we risk flattening out men's individual human experiences. We know not ALL men are inherently bad and we know everyone has a different life experience but we also can't deny there isn't some privilege from being perceived as a cis straight man in certain contexts, I've experienced it myself at various points in life. If we don't view the patriarchy as a power system that has oppressed us all for years (even straight cis men themselves) we forget the impact it's had on the world. If feminists didn't give us the language to identify and deconstruct the patriarchy, we'd all probably be making sourdough sandwiches right now.

We can all agree that the patriarchy is linked to heteronormativity, colonialism, capitalism, fetishisation, objectification. I could go on. But maybe I'll save that for my novel *Patriarchy: An Old Wives' Tale*, set in 2200.

We've seen how those that are viewed as 'other' are deemed less valuable in society and that's why you don't see any CEOs that look like me. That's why in 2021 only 37 CEOs of the Fortune 500 are women and only three of those 37 are women of colour. Gender inequality is still way behind when it comes to men and women, so how the hell are non-binary people supposed to get on top?

The real trick to life is to try and steer your own course. I like to think I have learned a few tricks along the way that might help you but I would never tell another person whose experience is different to mine how they should feel about anything. That's one of the many issues with people like Katie Hopkins or Piers Morgan. On the privilege scale they're pretty high up and yet they believe they speak for everyone. I don't think I speak for everyone but if anything in this book resonates or sticks with you, that's great. We can learn a thing or two by listening to others and in turn shift the power dynamics in public life and the media to be more inclusive and open. Having a singular story always pushed to the fore in culture creates stereotypes. That's why sharing my story with you is vital. That's why any trans, non-binary, gender nonconforming story being told is vital. It tells us that other people exist.

What fails us the most is not listening to each other and assuming that we are always right. I think this applies to all parts of life and not just gender. We all take up different spaces. We're all complicit in oppression somehow, whether it's because of our class or because we've been thrust into the spotlight by appearing on a TV show. I'm actively trying to do better by the people who haven't been given the same platform as me but who may have experienced the same struggles I have. Instead of striving for perfection we should seek liberation for ourselves and each other. There really is no end goal until there is an end goal for everybody. That's why having a PMA is important. You can't fight the good fight if you don't love yourself as well.

Gender is a lot like me throughout the years. Unstable. I say that as if I'm a fully functioning adult now but I still have moments where the art of being a failure takes hold and I'm seconds away from pressing the hot pink self-destruct button. Gender – like life itself – is fucking complex but it's fluid and that fluidity is okay.

Me and Kate Bornstein share a similar motto in life.

'Do whatever it takes to make your life more worth living, just don't be mean,'

It's that simple. Release the beast! Just don't be an areshole while you're doing it.

Love,
Bim x

Further Reading on Gender

Gender Outlaw and *Gender Outlaws: The Next Generation* by Kate Bornstein

Gender Trouble by Judith Butler

The Queer Art of Failure by Jack Halberstam

Life Isn't Binary by Meg-John Barker and Alex Iantaffi

Gender: A Graphic Guide by Meg-John Barker

They/Them/Their by Eris Young

In Their Shoes by Jamie Windust

Beyond the Gender Binary by Alok Vaid-Menon

Trans Like Me by CN Lester

How to Understand Your Gender by Meg-John Barker and Alex Iantaffi

Trans Power by Juno Roche

Stone Butch Blues by Leslie Feinberg

The Well of Loneliness by Radclyffe Hall

Man Enough to Be a Woman by Jayne County

Trans Britain by Christine Burns

The Transgender Issue by Shon Faye

Redefining Realness by Janet Mock

The Gender Games by Juno Dawson

Burgerz by Travis Alabanza

Life as a Unicorn by Amrou Al-Kadhi

Glossary of Gender Terminology

AFAB – Assigned Female At Birth

Ally – typically a straight and/or cis person who is supportive of the LGBTQ+ community

AMAB – Assigned Male At Birth

Cisgender – a person who identifies with their sex assignment at birth and the gender role associated with it

Gender – the system of meanings, social roles, stereotypes and expectations traditionally imposed on people due to their biological sex, but which can change according to culture and across time

Gender dysphoria – the clinical term used to describe feelings of distress with one's sex at birth, which may in some cases be alleviated by use of hormone therapy and surgery to reassign one's sex characteristics

Gender expression – the outward expression of masculinity, femininity or androgyny (or a mixture of these) through clothing, hair, makeup, name and pronouns

Gender identity – a person's deep sense of their own gender as being man, woman or something else (nonbinary), which may or may not accord with their sex assignment at birth

Gender nonconforming – a person whose gender expression subverts or does not meet the expectations associated with their gender identity or their assigned sex at birth

Genderqueer – an older term for 'non-binary', which some non-binary people may prefer to use about themselves

HRT – Hormone Replacement Therapy. The use of feminising oestrogen or masculinising testosterone to adjust one's body as part of a process of transition

Non-binary – an umbrella term to describe people whose gender identity is different from their assigned sex at birth, but who do not straightforwardly identify as men or women either

Pronouns – words used to describe someone who is being talked about. In English, third person pronouns indicate the gender of the person being discussed through use of 'he' or 'she'. 'They' is also used when a person's gender is unknown and many non-binary people use 'they' as a neutral pronoun to indicate they are neither male nor female

Sex – classification as male/female based on one's biological characteristics at birth

Trans – an umbrella term for those whose gender identity differs from, is not the same as or does not sit comfortably with the sex they were assigned at birth

Transgender – a person whose gender identity differs from their sex assignment at birth and the gender role associated with it. 'Trans' is now the more common term

Trans man – a man who was assigned female at birth

Trans woman – a woman who was assigned male at birth

Transition – any social or medical steps a person may take to be more widely recognised as their gender identity. This could include changing dress, hair, pronouns and names, but can also mean use of hormones and surgery to change their physical characteristics

Resources

UK Nationwide Organisations and Charities

Action for Trans Health
Working to improve trans people's access to healthcare.
www.actionfortranshealth.org.uk

Albert Kennedy Trust (AKT)
Support for LGBTQ+ young people facing or experiencing homelessness.
www.akt.org.uk

Allsorts Youth Project
Brighton-based organisation that listens to, supports and connects LGBTQ+ children and young people under 26.
www.allsortsyouth.org.uk

AZ Magazine
Online publication for LGBTQ+ people of colour, creating a voice for those who have felt excluded from the wider LGBTQ+ community.
www.azmagazine.co.uk

Ban Conversion Therapy (UK)
A coalition of LGBTQIA+ communities and organisations calling for the government to ban conversion therapy.
www.banconversiontherapy.com

BBZ London

Bold Brazen Zamis or Babes are a curatorial and creative production collective from south-east London, prioritising the experiences of queer womxn, trans folk and non-binary people of colour.
www.bbzblkbk.com

Black LGBTQIA+ Therapy Fund

Program to fund therapy sessions for Black LGBTQIA+ folk with the aim to make therapy more accessible.
www.blacklgbtfund.com

Blackout UK

Not-for-profit social enterprise run by a volunteer collective working to mobilise Black gay/bi and/or trans men to address shared challenges and build spaces and networks.
www.blkoutuk.com

Black Trans Alliance

Non-profit organisation supporting Black trans and non-binary people in London and the wider community.
www.blacktransalliance.org

Black Trans Foundation

Not-for-profit organisation based in the UK, working to build a world where Black trans people have the same access to healthcare and opportunities as their cisgender counterparts.
Email: blacktransfoundation@gmail.com

Books Beyond Bars UK

Collective of volunteers who send books and other educational materials to incarcerated LGBTQIA+ people across the UK.
www.beyond-bars.org

Deaf LGBTIQA

Website where deaf people can find information and resources on the deaf LGBTIQA+ community in an accessible way.
www.deaflgbtiqa.org.uk

ELOP

Innovative lesbian and gay mental health charity based in East London.
www.elop.org

Equality Network

National charity working for LGBTI equality and human rights in Scotland.
www.equality-network.org

FFLAG

Voluntary organisation dedicated to supporting parents and families and their LGBT+ members.
www.fflag.org.uk

Galop

LGBT+ anti-abuse charity working with and for LGBT+ victims and survivors of interpersonal abuse and violence.
www.galop.org.uk

Gendered Intelligence

Charity that aims to increase understandings of gender diversity and improve trans people's quality of life.
www.genderedintelligence.co.uk

Gender Swap

UK initiative supporting trans and gender nonconforming individuals to access clothes and community.
www.genderswap.org

GIRES UK

UK-wide organisation whose purpose is to improve the lives of trans and gender diverse people of all ages, including those who are non-binary and non-gender.
www.gires.org.uk

Imaan

The UK's leading LGBTQ Muslim charity, working to help reconcile faith with sexuality and gender identity.
www.imaanlondon.wordpress.com

Intersex UK

Organisation by and for intersex people in the UK and Ireland, working to protect the bodily autonomy and civil rights of intersex children, adolescents and their families.
www.facebook.com/intersexuk

Just Like Us UK

LGBT+ young people's charity seeking to empower young people to champion LGBT+ equality.
www.justlikeus.org

LGBT Consortium

National infrastructure and membership organisation, working to strengthen and support LGBTQ+ groups, organisations and projects.

www.consortium.lgbt

LGBT Foundation

National charity delivering advice, support and information services to LGBT communities.

www.lgbt.foundation

LGBT+ Switchboard

Provides a one-stop listening service for LGBT+ people on the phone, by email and through instant messaging.

www.switchboard.lgbt

London Friend

The UK's oldest LGBT charity, supporting the health and mental wellbeing of the LGBT community in and around London.

www.londonfriend.org.uk

London LGBTQ+ Community Centre

Their goal is to set up a safe, sober, intergenerational community centre and café for the LGBTQ+ community of London.

www.londonlgbtqcentre.org

Mermaids UK

Support for transgender, non-binary and gender-diverse children, young people and their families.

www.mermaidsuk.org.uk

Mindline Trans+

Mental health support helpline for anyone identifying as transgender, non-binary or genderfluid, including their family members, friends, colleagues and carers.

www.mindlinetrans.org.uk

MindOut

Mental health service run by and for LGBTQ+ people.

www.mindout.org.uk

Mosaic Trust

Youth group that supports, educates and inspires young LGBT+ people and those around them.

www.mosaictrust.org.uk

National Trans Youth Network

Network of trans youth groups across the UK.

www.ntyn.org.uk

Not A Phase

Small charity supporting the lives of trans+ adults across the UK

www.notaphase.org

Opening Doors London

Charity connecting LGBTQ+ people over 50 with activities, events, support and information.

www.openingdoorslondon.org.uk

The Outside Project

London's LGBTIQ+ community shelter, centre and domestic abuse refuge.

www.lgbtiqoutside.org

Papyrus

National charity dedicated to the prevention of young suicide.

www.papyrus-uk.org

Pink Therapy

UK's largest independent therapy organisation working with gender and sexual diversity clients.

www.pinktherapy.com

Press For Change

The UK's leading experts in transgender law, focusing on the rights and treatment of trans people.

www.pfc.org.uk

The Proud Trust

Organisation that helps LGBT+ young people empower themselves, to make a positive change for themselves and their communities.

www.theproudtrust.org

Queer Britain

Charity working to establish the UK's first national LGBTQ+ museum.

www.queerbritain.org.uk

Queer Futures

National study investigating the self-harm and suicide of LGBTQ youth.

www.queerfutures.co.uk

RUComingOut

Website with resources and helpful time on coming out.

www.rucomingout.com

Rainbow Grow

Hackney-based LGBTQI+ community gardening initiative.
www.rainbowgrowhackney.wordpress.com

Rainbow Mind

Collaborative project aiming to tackle mental health issues within the LGBTQI+ community across Greater Manchester and London
www.rainbowmind.org

Rainbow Noir

Manchester-based peer support and community action group, which celebrates and platforms people of colour who identify as LGBTQI.
www.rainbownoirmcr.com

Scottish Trans Alliance

Working to improve gender identity and gender reassignment equality, rights and inclusion in Scotland.
www.scottishtrans.org

Sisters Uncut

Feminist direct action group that is opposed to cuts to UK government services for domestic violence victims.
www.sistersuncut.org

Spectra London

Offering non-judgmental, accessible services and support to marginalised and disadvantaged communities in London, with a focus on sexual health and emotional wellbeing.
www.spectra-london.org.uk

Stonewall
Campaigning and lobbying group.
www.stonewall.org.uk

Stonewall Housing
Works to ensure LGBT people live in safer homes, free from fear.
www.stonewallhousing.org

Sylvia Rivera Law Project
Working to guarantee that all people are free to self-determine gender identity and expression, regardless of income or race.
www.srlp.org

Terrence Higgins Trust
The UK's leading HIV and sexual health charity, providing services to and campaigning on HIV issues.
www.tht.org.uk

Trans Pride Brighton
The first and largest Trans Pride event outside of the US, whose aim is to inspire all trans, intersex, gender variant and queer people to help make a difference.
www.transpridebrighton.org

Trans Unite
Comprehensive resource for people in the UK searching for support in the transgender community.
www.transunite.co.uk

The Trevor Project

Leading national organisation providing crisis intervention and suicide prevention to LGBTQ+ young people.
www.thetrevorproject.org

UK Black Pride

Europe's largest celebration for LGBTQI+ people of African, Asian, Caribbean, Latin American and Middle Eastern descent.
www.ukblackpride.org.uk

Voices4 London

Aims to aid protests, share knowledge and skills and create a safe queer family and space for vulnerable people.
www.voices4london.org.uk

We Exist

Trans-led organisation working to provide more spaces for trans people to platform their work and ideas and discuss issues affecting their community.
www.weexist.co.uk

International Organisations and Charities

African Rainbow Family

Not-for-profit charitable organisation that supports LGBTIQ people of African heritage and the wider BAME groups.
www.africanrainbowfamily.org

All Out

A global movement and campaigning group fighting to stop LBGT+ people being imprisoned or tortured because of who they are or who they love.

www.allout.org

Black Queer Travel Guide

Digital resource offering experiences, safety advice and information to Black queer travellers around the globe.

www.theblackqueertravelguide.com

GLAAD

As a dynamic media force, US-based GLAAD tackles tough issues to shape the narrative and provoke dialogue, rewriting the script for LGBTQ acceptance.

www.glaad.org

Kaleidoscope Trust

UK-based charity fighting for the human rights of LGBTQ+ people across the world.

www.kaleidoscopetrust.com

Acknowledgements

Is this the part of the book where I pretend I'm giving an Oscars speech? If so, so cue me becoming a blubbering Olivia Colman as she accepted her Academy Award.

Writing a book has always been a dream of mine. Did I think I was going to go on *Drag Race* and then write a book straight away? No, but I bloody well did it. My life changed dramatically after appearing on that show, in a way that I am truly grateful for. Since March 2021, life has become a whirlwind; I feel like my feet haven't touched the ground and somehow I have still managed to Release the Beast and become a Bimini Bon Book Author. It's crazy.

I wanna say thanks to Penguin for being like, 'yeah, alright, let's do a book with Bim'. It means a lot as a queer artist to be able to share my thoughts in a form that's going to be there forever. Yikes.

I want to say thanks to my editors Tom Killingbeck and Susannah Bennett for truly fighting for this opportunity and believing I had enough to say to push for this book to be written. As hectic as my life has been, somehow we still managed to put this book together in record time. GO US!

The book also wouldn't have been complete without the constant support and guidance of Shon Faye. She helped break down my thoughts and tell me if I was rambling (which happened a lot). We started out with a few relaxed Zooms, where I would lay on my leopard-print chaise-longue. But she was soon leaving me sexy voice notes of giggling hysteria and 'it's gonna be okay' reassurance when I felt like my world was gonna implode. I couldn't have written this without Shon. She is the moment, come on now.

Being on *Drag Race* changed my life. I'm gagged that I stayed true to myself and some people seemed to like me. Wild. It's the art of failure coming through again. I've felt like an imposter a lot of times throughout my life and being thrust into the public eye didn't come without those feelings. I want to say thanks to *Drag Race* and also the people post-show that have supported me, bought this book, commented on my posts and come to my shows. I have so many ideas in store and I hope I can make you all proud.

To my mum, I love you. Thank you for supporting me even when it was confusing. I understand that social politics made it difficult to understand why I wanted to wear a wig and a dress, and it didn't help that voices in our small town were deafening. You stood by me and told people you were proud when you were probably embarrassed, but look where we are now. I took you for dinner at the Shard. Made it!

To Ray, Henry, Lillia, Mark, Michelle, William and Freddy. My family who support me even when I'm wearing an outfit you might deem stupid, thank you.

To my Grandad. He's 81 and he came and watched a show of mine recently that had drag kings, trans performers, AFAB performers, me gyrating on a chair and he still laughed and enjoyed it. Thank you for being open-minded. I know Granny would have been proud and we all love and miss her so much.

To Ella Lynch, my creative partner. Your genius and talent is unmatched and I love everything we do together. You truly are a dream and I am so lucky to have you in my life. Here's to many more exhibitions and iconic looks together.

To Profile Talent for trusting me to make the right decisions and for all the incredible opportunities that have come my way.

Thank you to Next Management for taking a risk and believing that my face could be in a fashion magazine. We shot *Vogue Italia* and all the other editorials and I can't wait to see what's to come!

To Simon Jones. You got my mug on multiple magazines . . . Thanks for believing in me and for always keeping my name in the press. I can't wait to see what else we do in the world!

Thanks to THE Róisín Murphy for making me look beautiful on the cover of this book, and to Byron London for beating my mug and for all the work we have done and will continue to do.

To my darling Stefano. You've seen me at my worst and still stood by me. You even kissed me when my eyebrows were halfway up my forehead. Thank you for being on this path with me. I love you.

To E. It hasn't been easy for us over the years, but time is a healer and I wish that one day we will be as close again as we once were. You were a big part of my life and I cherish all our memories.

All my mates. I won't write individual names here, but for everyone who has impacted my life in any way, thank you. From the bottom of my glittery heart. Those who were with me before drag, when I was a queer in Yarmouth, partying in London, wearing rubbish outfits or had that weird monobrow club kid moment – thanks for not deserting me.

Most importantly, I'd like to dedicate this book to my best friend Ellie Tweed. We may not be together on this plane now, but I know you're watching over everyone you loved, smiling away with that gorgeous grin. Your kindness and compassion continues to inspire me whenever I feel like it's too much. I wish I could share this journey I've been on with you, but I know you're by my side. You're watching over us all. You taught me more than you could ever realise and I can't wait to dance with you again. Until then, I hope I make you proud. Love ya bab. Skinny bitch X.

That's me off. I'm in Devon right now. Was meant to be on a two-day holiday but I took my eye off the book deadline. It's hard being pretty and smart.

If you've read this book, thank you. I'm a human sharing my own experiences and I don't know all the answers. I never claimed to, either. This is all my crazy little brain talking honestly and openly about my experiences with sexuality, gender and identity. If this has helped even one of you in your own experience, that's good enough for me.

Love you all,
Bimini x